Boats without Oars:

Ancient-Future Evangelism, an American Road trip, and collected stories from the Episcopal Church

KRISTIN AND MICHAEL CARROCCINO

For permissions or requests, please contact: www.carroccinocollective.com.

Printed in the United States of America

First Printing, 2014

ISBN: 978-1503121492

Interior Design: Kristin Carroccino and Michael Carroccino.

FOR CAEDMON AND MIRELLA

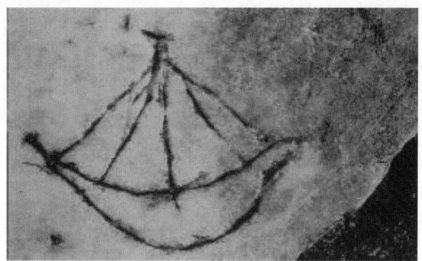

Early Christian boat symbol representing the church
from the Catacombs of St. Callixtus outside Rome.

Mystical Icon of the Holy Church, iconographer Matthew Garrett, 2008.
http://www.holy-icons.com

"TWENTY YEARS FROM NOW YOU WILL BE MORE DISAPPOINTED BY THE THINGS THAT YOU DIDN'T DO THAN BY THE ONES YOU DID DO. SO THROW OFF THE BOWLINES. SAIL AWAY FROM THE SAFE HARBOR. CATCH THE TRADE WINDS IN YOUR SAILS. EXPLORE. DREAM. DISCOVER."

—MARK TWAIN

"THE BOAT CAME BREASTING OUT OF THE MIST, AND IN THEY STEPPED. ALL NEW THINGS IN LIFE WERE MEANT TO COME LIKE THAT."

—EUDORA WELTY

You must be this fish
that the waves
of the world
do not swallow you

Photo: Kristin Carroccino. Block print by Kellura Johnson.

"Imitate that fish, which although it received less grace, should be a marvel to you. It is in the sea and over the waves; it is in the sea and swims above the tide. On the sea, the tempest rages, hurricanes roar, but the fish swims. Similarly, this world is a sea to you. It has varying currents, huge surges, and fierce gales. And you must be a fish, so that the waves of the world cannot drown you."[1]
—Ambrose

---

[1] Robin M. Jensen. *Baptismal Imagery in Early Christianity: Ritual, Visual and Theological Dimensions.* (Baker Books, June 1, 2012), pp. 72-73.

CONTENTS

Image: Public domain.

The process of writing *Boats without Oars* is the sort of story best told gathered around a campfire, staring into embers, laughing occasionally, and contemplating the stars. Like the lives of the ancient Celtic missionaries Michael and I are still reading about, and like the stories of many of the people we met in the summer of 2012 on our road trip, the tale is complicated. Replete with twists, turns, and large swaths of frustrating, stagnant months and setbacks, this is a very human story. Here, there is adventure, drama, comedy, tension, and romance.

When we returned home to Texas from our venture two years ago, I envisioned translating the *Boats without Oars* blog into a manuscript within a few months, then submitting drafts to publishers. I did not picture the intervening years between then and now: how Michael's graduation from seminary, a cross-country move, parenting two children, publishing two additional books, one of us beginning a new career and the other pursuing a calling more deeply, might affect my tidy and in-control publication timeline. Most of all, I wasn't prepared to understand how *Boats without Oars* needed to settle for a time to allow Michael and me to begin to integrate the experiences we had that summer as individuals, as family members, and as Episcopalians. The book you hold now and the stories within are richer because of the waiting.

This collection is the result of consolidating, contemplating, wrestling with, and expanding upon the experiences we had in 2012. We decided to maintain the basic structure we created on the *Boats without Oars* blog: between March and August 2012, Michael and I blogged about church and evangelism, then invited "guest bloggers" to contribute their ideas. Following our return to Texas that August, we converted the blog posts to essays and revised portions of our writing. More recently, we added updates from the churches we visited for the project and questions for individual or small group use. We also decided to include more of our family stories about "life on the road." We wrote the last section of *Boats without Oars* during the autumn of 2014, which allowed us time to reflect more deeply on our 2012 experiences.

Michael and I created this resource to preserve the narratives that seven Episcopal churches across the United States were telling in 2012 and to contain the stories we made as a family. Our hope is that *Boats without Oars* will help to foster conversations about evangelism and encourage church communities of all sizes to begin asking questions about where they find themselves and what they see on the horizon. **—Kristin**

I learned in seminary that the primary language of theology—the closest we get to describing God—is prayer. I learned from *Boats without Oars* that our prayer derives meaning from an even deeper source: story. This book is a story. It is subjective. It is contextual. For most of the last two years, I could only envision this project as a fully cross-referenced, footnoted, peer-reviewed, in-depth exposition of describable results and implications from narrative comparison across a series of parishes (!). With charts and tables. Perhaps I will write that book one day, but for now, this is the story that I need to tell. On the road in 2012, and in the countless hours of compiling and editing this material, I have seen the Holy Spirit at work.

Boats without Oars began in the midst of a transitional time. During my seminary education, my family was attending a different church than I was. Our children, Caedmon and Mirella, were unaccustomed to seeing me in front of the church instead of beside them in the pews. I was no longer a layperson and not yet a priest. I thought of this project as a purely academic endeavor, isolated from the reality of spending several months on the road having a great time.

The summer of 2012 began the process of healing some of those divisions. Today, I am not quite so eager to carve up and tabulate the results of my interviews, develop a "narrative taxonomy" that informs a theory of the relationship between story themes and church vitality, or separate the experiences we had as a family on a road trip from our church research. This collection of stories and reflections—from my family, from people in churches all over the country, from dozens of fellow travelers—is an exercise in a more primal kind of theology.

The future of the church, the story God is telling, the work of the Holy Spirit: all are bound up inextricably in the deepest parts of every person making the journey. There is no sanitized and segregated system for engaging the Holy Spirit. *Boats without Oars* is an invitation to embark on a voyage of discovery. Hoist your sail and join us. The deep waters beckon. **—Michael**

LAUNCH!

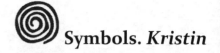

Emblazoned with their love of God, fearless in their desire to follow the Spirit, early Celtic missionaries pushed off from the shore in tiny boats called coracles, sometimes even with no oars, determined to flourish and share the Good News wherever their wayward boat next landed. These are ancient stories from the era of St. Patrick of Ireland, St. Columba of Iona, and of Celtic missionaries encountered by Alfred the Great. The fantastic idea of sailing off on a boat with no oars on the winds of the Spirit is also in the book of Isaiah—"There the LORD will be our Mighty One. It will be like a place of broad rivers and streams. No galley with oars will ride them, no mighty ship will sail them" (v. 33:21)—or in the pursuit of romance in the tale of *Tristan and Isolde:*[2]

ISOLT SIGNALS TO TRISTRAM

Now Tristan knew there was no cure for him in Cornwall. But his heart told him to go to sea and seek there either healing or death. 'I would like to try the sea that brings all chances...I would have the sea bear me far off alone, to what land, no matter, so that it will heal me of my wound. And perchance someday I will once more serve you, fair uncle, as your harper, your huntsman, and your liege.'

---

[2] This image is found on http://www.ancientworlds.net/aw/Post/1296600 and is a facsimile of one of several tiles found at Chertsey Abbey. Monks carved the images around 1270. The tiles are now held by the British Museum.

They laid him gently in a small boat, without sail or oars. He left his sword on the shore, for it could no longer help him. But he took his harp into the boat for comfort on the way. Then, with tears, they pushed him out to sea and committed him to God. And the sea drew him away...[3]

These ancient tales capture our modern hearts. Why? Whether speaking of ourselves as individuals or examining the state of the modern church, I think we most often imagine ourselves as being stuck on the shore, stuck in the moment, unsure of how to get from here to there, of how to really connect with people and authentically share our faith. The idea of cutting the line and releasing ourselves, our churches and communities, to the lure of the waves on the horizon, the gust of wind, to God to set us off, is mesmerizing and sometimes terrifying. "To give up the oar and sail means to drop personal control and give oneself over to the will of God."[4]

We chose the image of "boats without oars" to symbolize a new way of thinking about mission—a new way of being—of being ready to be sent. Of being brave. Of listening deeply and trusting. During our *Boats without Oars* journey in 2012, Michael and I and our children set off on a mission to meet with Episcopal communities launching themselves from church as we've known it—from a paradigm that has seemed safe and secure—into new territory. We wanted to find out why some of us choose to stay on the shore or perhaps even walk away from the ocean, while others step into the boat and set sail.

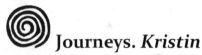 Journeys. *Kristin*

Michael and I started our journey together over twelve years ago—seeking refuge in each other and on the road—in search of learning, bowing at the feet of our teachers: the wild mountain vistas, thundering waterfalls, smooth-as-glass rivers gliding beneath our canoe. Certain people were guides: a couple of evangelical pastors, the self-proclaimed "crazy Indian" guy, several groups of "at-risk" teenaged-boys, Sous-chefs, book nerds, artists, a self-identifying hermit, and a lot of church people. Being in wild places and worshipping in church communities shaped our shared spirituality, and our "church journey" was as meandering as many of the hiking trails we've trekked: departing from deep family roots in the

---

[3] Robert A. Johnson. *We: Understanding the Psychology of Romantic Love.* (San Francisco: Harper & Row, 1983), p. 14.
[4] ibid, p. 33.

Southern Baptist Church, spending about three weeks experiencing Pentecostalism, wandering for a couple of years in Non-Denominationalism until finding our home in the Episcopal Church.

In the middle of winter 2012, we were in a quandary. Many of Michael's classmates at the Seminary were preparing for far-flung summer adventures in places like Africa and Guatemala, busy applying for grants and scholarships. Others were looking forward to a summer spent in their home state or country, working at summer camps and taking a well-deserved break from academic rigor. For various reasons, including a seminarian's budget and having two children, ages four and six at the time, we were looking for a different sort of experience. One that didn't include remaining in Austin, Texas, and enduring one more summer of the long drought that had begun shortly after we moved to the campus of the Seminary of the Southwest in August 2010. We had relocated to Austin that year from Bellingham, Washington, for Michael to begin pursuing a master of divinity with hopes of graduating in 2013 and becoming ordained as a priest in the Episcopal Church.

We began to think like many nostalgic and travel-loving Americans with a summer laid out long before us: "road trip!" but we wanted something more than the delight of exploration and discovery that a good road trip offers. We wanted to learn more about the church that we were continually being called into as a family. We wanted to know why some Episcopal churches were shrinking and closing and others thriving. Being a prospective "clergy spouse," I was curious to observe how other people lived into that role—or didn't.

We started planning. Over the next couple of months, we applied for grants, contacted bishops, priests, and friends all across the United States and asked if they knew of any churches in their area that were growing and "doing things differently." Pretty quickly we developed some qualifications for the churches we were interested in studying: we were looking for small- to medium-sized churches who were growing and perhaps even growing by thinking "outside of the box." Having both grown up as Southern Baptists, complete with experiences of going door-to-door to invite people to church and observing pastors give weekly, passionate "altar calls," we were also curious to learn what Episcopalians thought about evangelism.

Before we knew it, we had learned how to create a blog and had started to foster a virtual conversation about evangelism in the Episcopal Church. Michael began working with one of his professors to develop an academic study based on

Narrative Leadership,[5] a subject he enjoyed in his seminary classes, to lend structure to our adventure. The weeks flew by, and suddenly, we were standing in our driveway in May, having locked the door to our house with no plans to return until mid-August. Writing about Celtic evangelists, Jeri Ballast captures how we felt in that moment:

> Most did not know where they were headed when their journey began, nor what hardships they might endure along the way. They traveled light, trusting in providence to provide for their needs and trusting God to take them where they were to go. It is the pilgrimage itself that defines who we are; the journey is the purifying fire. God alone determines where, when, and how that journey ends. What we offer to God is our willingness to step out onto the path and start walking.[6]

 **Peregrination.** *Michael*

Boats without Oars began with a big, blank calendar and a passion for peregrination: we love journeys of all kinds, both the internal and the external. Kristin and I have been traveling together for well over a decade, and we have logged many thousands of miles in our pursuit to discover and be delighted by God, one another, and ourselves. Peregrination is a word like pilgrimage, but with larger implications. Ancient Celtic monks saw the spiritual life as a peregrination, a series of pilgrimages both inner and outer; our outer travels reflect and embody our inner searching.

Embracing spiritual peregrination, some Celtic monks, like St. Brendan or St. Columba, would depart their comfortable and familiar world with a combination of meditative and delirious sensibilities: they would climb into tiny boats (occasionally without even an oar) and let the wind and currents carry them on the cold North Atlantic. As they tested their faith and ability to survive harrowing

---

[5] Narrative Leadership is a practice whereby leaders look and listen for stories with themes of success, hope, strength, overcoming challenge, etc., within their organization, then use those stories to build unifying identity and mission for the community. Fluency in their understanding of narrative function determines how such leaders interpret challenges, communicate ideas, and present themselves and their companies.

[6] The essay from which this passage is excerpted is printed in full in the last section of this book. Jerri Ballast, http://www.heartoscotland.com/Categories/CelticChristianity.htm, 2002.

conditions, they knew that when they landed, they were where God intended them to be both in geographical location and in spiritual disposition.

Over the course of months of planning and always holding in the backs of our minds the stories of the Celts, we slowly settled on a project involving Episcopalians and stories, and specifically an exploration of the radically different nature of evangelism in a religious culture that all but shuns the word. Episcopalians evangelize, but not in the classical American understanding of the term. We researched, planned, traveled, and listened to stories of the Episcopal Church, then spent time writing and reflecting about the collective experiences of our peregrinations.

Boats without Oars displays a classic narrative arc progressing from mild questioning to deep unsettling as our understanding of the project changed. By the end of our summer travels in August 2012, we were only beginning to draw the disparate narrative threads together in a vague understanding of what we had done. Our epic road trip and research became more a story than a simple project over the course of its life and changed us in unexpected ways.

Our book offers stories about ourselves and the Episcopal Church that both inspire and sometimes disturb, and each is a part of the big, complex, multi-layered, chaotic, and beautiful organism we like to think of as the Body of Christ. You might begin to notice the winds shifting, the currents changing, the sky clearing. The boat, after all, is the church, and we are collectively doing our best to turn the sails into the wind of the Spirit. Maybe none of us needs oars after all...

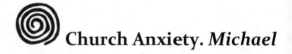 # Church Anxiety. *Michael*

The anxiety in the air is palpable. Every time I read about the current state of the Episcopal Church, I see phrases like, "the writing is on the wall" or, "the aging church" or, "mainline decline." In response, we hear stories of church plants aimed at (and filled with) young people or of large urban churches with the financial heft to try bold new things. Websites, magazines, and church leaders repeatedly present these as visions of our church's future. Often left out of the exciting prose and glossy pictures, however, is the plain fact that such examples are far outside the scale of the vast majority of parishes. What is to become of the rest of us?

There are so many vibrant and friendly churches out there. Though thriving and energetic, their average age continues to creep up a little each year. They cannot birth a new and separate congregation without undermining the community, nor do they have capacity to develop the kind of resource-intensive programs that draw in families with young children or entice young postmoderns to enter the building. These churches know that change is coming—they know the future looks different—but have few ideas about how to get there from here. This "church anxiety" served as the catalyst for *Boats without Oars*.

At its heart, *Boats without Oars* is a conversation: in 2012, we sought out churches across the country whose stories could provide a counterpoint to the narrative of "mainline decline." Our central thesis was simple and clear: we believe that the seeds of the future are contained in the stories we tell today. We wanted to understand the challenges facing congregations by collecting literary snapshots of intergenerational communities that are thriving in a landscape of uncertainty, and then to share those stories as broadly as possible. We set out to explore what the future may hold for the thousands of local Episcopal churches throughout our nation, and to shed light on what the Holy Spirit is doing to grow our church and move us forward into the future.

Join us on this journey: imagine your stories, hopes, dreams, and fears. You are standing on the shore, waiting to launch, what do you see on the horizon?

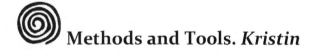 **Methods and Tools. *Kristin***

Research, writing, and planning occupied a lot of our time in the months leading up to the launch of our heavily laden car out of our hot Texan driveway with a travelling schedule that unfurled delectably before us like an exotic scavenger hunt. Michael studied Narrative Theory[7] and devised sets of questions to ask our study participants. We procured a voice recorder and more memory for our laptop computer. We devised a structure for the blog: I would write about my impressions of the communities we were visiting: Did a locale affect one church more than another did? Were churches in the Deep South doing things differently than in the Pacific Northwest? Michael would compile the interviews gathered

---

[7] Narrative Theory is based on the assumption that narrative—or storytelling—is the primary tool for human interpretation of reality. By studying stories, their constituent elements (plot, character, etc.) and themes (tragedy, defiance, etc.), their use, and their structures, narratologists draw conclusions about the ways in which people create meaning and perceive the world.

from students, parishioners, and clergy, and reflect on his findings. We would invite the study participants to share their thoughts about the Episcopal Church and evangelism.

Other tools? Those tended to be a bit more tactile: camping equipment, a jar of coins for Laundromats, an iPad, over-the-car-seat organizers and lap desks for the kids, fresh sets of colored pencils, many books, a cooler, and a big dose of optimism and curiosity.

MARCH 2012:
SETTING OUR
SIGHTS

In March, we had many questions to answer: was this journey possible? Would our car endure thousands of road miles? Did we need to sublet our rental house? Would the Seminary and our Bishop support our efforts? How would we get along with each other over all of those traveling hours? Many of these questions created expected anxiety, but there were questions that probed deeper: If we take this journey, what sorts of churches will we visit? Do Episcopalians really care about evangelism? How might this journey change us?

The answers to some questions only created more. With each step forward in our planning, unexpected opportunities and decisions arose. This early process of discernment materially shaped *Boats without Oars* and determined what it might become. From this initial phase sprang what would become our foundational question for the research side of our journey: what is "evangelism?"

We posed this question to small groups of students, friends, seminary professors, and members of our church communities. Then, we started the *Boats without Oars* blog to broadcast our inquiry. The blog—and its fundamental question about evangelism—gathered enough interest and skepticism to assure us that our journey was worth taking and our questions worth asking.

—Kristin and Michael

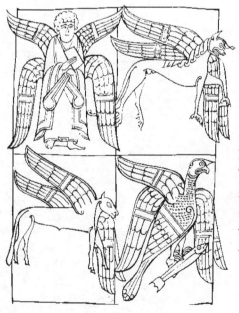

Public domain reproduction of "living creatures" in the Gospels from the Ninth-Century Celtic Book of Armagh in Trinity College, Dublin. For further reading about early symbols of evangelism, see: www.fatherwatson.livejournal.com/69844.html.

Evangelism. *Michael*

Lately Kristin and I have been attending an evening class at St. David's Episcopal Church, a large, thriving parish in downtown Austin, Texas. This unique class is well attended, and by people with a broad range of demographics and church attendance patterns. The student body looks like what we think church generally should—eager participants from all walks of life gathering together. There is, however, one rather significant departure from church norms: our class has no specifically named Christian content. The class is entitled "Cultivating Forgiveness," and our teacher is a Jewish woman with decades of training in Buddhist meditation.

Why would St. David's allow such a marked—and unsettling—omission? Clearly, this church has touched upon a collective yearning by offering this class. People across the spectrum sense a deep need for practical teaching about how to live into what is, after all, a very Christian concept: forgiveness. This is risky; how does the church navigate in a pluralistically muddied world with very intense spiritual needs, yet maintain its unique identity as centered in Christ? This is not about increasing worship attendance or making converts in our image; it is about providing the larger community with a meaningful connection to the divine, regardless of their spiritual status. We have a term for this kind of work: *evangelism.*

Evangelism is a word we tend to shy away from in the Episcopal Church. It has been too often reappropriated in societal language to denote a stance of spiritual imperialism—the church asserting itself as the sole arbiter of truth and reality. Christians can no longer assume a general familiarity with our faith. Often, in fact, quite the opposite is true: our society puts us on the defensive in matters of belief. The cynicism that suffuses our culture is apt to view Christian claims of redemption, celebration, and gratitude as just another sales pitch: a veiled attempt to gain power and wealth. Far from inspiring others and providing meaningful connection, evangelism, so defined, serves only to further alienate the church from society. This is hardly "Good News."

However, evangelism is nothing like the description we have unwittingly adopted from its detractors. Evangelism is not about getting more people into the building, nor is it about converting people to an understanding of God that perfectly mirrors my own. (A seminary professor of mine recently said, "the shadow side of religion is my need for you to believe what I believe, so that I can believe what I believe is believable.") Evangelism is about finding where God is already at work, whether in a community or in an individual human heart, and joining in. While church membership in America may be declining over time, God is still very much at work in every human heart. How can your church join in that work?

Winning Souls. *Kristin*

If evangelism is a journey to join God where God is already working, then the first and most intimate place we experience transformation is in our souls. We know our soul, that expansive interior castle, in those moments we feel most fully alive: on a mountaintop, in a courtroom making a first-class persuasive argument, tucking our children into bed and kissing sweetly sleeping cheeks, harvesting a perfectly ripe tomato, or creating the perfect turn of phrase. Finding and winning our soul, and thus encountering God, is a different experience for each person. Indeed, over a lifetime of soul-searching and basking in those moments of love, one finds God more and more often, equally joyful viewing a vast sunset vista as a carefully washed dish in the kitchen sink.

In my desire that all may realize the peace of God, what does "winning souls" (in the phrase used more commonly in the parlance of my Southern Baptist roots) mean to me today and to the greater Episcopal Church community to which I now belong? I think evangelism begins with conveying to people that they *have* a soul, that it's as real as the skin over their bones and must be tended to at least as fervently as pursuing healthy eating or physical exercise (and that indeed even *those* practices are expressions of soul, of the unique imprint of God in each individual). We will either spend time tending to our inner cathedrals or ignore them and place their care outside of ourselves, inviting disappointment and chaos.

One way to tend the soul is to immerse into a community engaged in soul work— a church, for example—with each community expressing this quest in a unique way. If the practice of communal soul care is unappealing for a time, then one might find a practice of soul care individually, perhaps through meditation or prayer. I say "for a time," because tending to the soul is almost impossible to sustain for long in isolation. We humans yearn for each other, to shine the reflection of our souls on anyone around who is ready to bask in its radiance. When I pick that perfectly ripe tomato from a garden I've lovingly tended all spring, photograph it, and upload that photo to Facebook to share my joy, and my friends "like" it, my online community has seen a glimpse of God working and living through me, through my joys and passions, my soul.

Being made of skin, hair, and teeth, I think even the best online communities will not nourish my soul over the long haul. So I choose to tend to my soul in a community that meets at least weekly to physically receive the mysterious elements of the body and blood of Christ, kneeling together at a common table in unity despite whatever neighborly issues we've been struggling through over the past week. In those moments, we are all soul mates immersed in a fantastic, often inexplicable love.

Evangelism, then, is winning souls. Not in the old hellfire-and-brimstone guilt sort-of way, but in being deeply present to the people around us: really looking at our spouse across the room, seeing a coworker, client, panhandler, and reminding each other that we all have souls, and that God is in our midst.

Photo credit: Kristin Carroccino. Impromptu Eucharist, Indiana July 2012.

Incense and Soccer Balls. *Michael*

In the spring of 2012, Samuel Wells visited the Seminary of the Southwest as a guest lecturer. He chose to talk about the extreme importance of a single commonly used preposition: *with*. In several engaging stories, he presented a modern church which understands its mission primarily in the context of doing things *for* (rather than *with*) people outside the church. Instead of operating from the commonly accepted norm that all ministries are mutually beneficial, the structures and norms of our regular practices of service to the poor and needy assume a distinct separation between the minister and those to whom he or she ministers. Wells astutely observed that such a system ultimately ends in dysfunction, because in doing something *for* another, we understand ourselves as being different than (and thus superior to) those whom we serve. These separations hinder our ability to empathize with their physical and spiritual needs as fellow human beings. Ministry, according Wells, must be a "with," not a "for."

During the questions that followed, Wells illuminated another group of outsiders: visitors who wish to join our churches. Often, the church takes a programmatic approach to initiation that assumes we are providing something *for* the newcomers. When asked how he welcomes people into the church in ways that maintain this new paradigm, Wells' response was fantastic in its simplicity and broad application. He operates with the understanding that each person already has a working familiarity with worship and theology, and the incorporating work of the church is to discover those unique resources in every individual and celebrate them. Thus for new members (sometimes referred to as catechumens), Wells uses a very simple set of questions to discover and appreciate their innate spiritual character.

Four Questions for Catechumens:

What is your favorite part of the liturgy?

Why?

Where else do you find this in your week?

What does this tell you about God?

Wells' stories of employing these questions are delightful. He once heard a soccer fan compare the mystical quality created by incense in worship to the enormous feeling of spiritual connection he feels in the crowded terraces of a Manchester United soccer game. From a single observation, this "uninitiated" Christian came to the profound conclusion that God is an immense mystery that we experience primarily in unity with others. Wells did not have to do anything *for* that man, yet gained a great deal by staying *with* him as he found the words to express a unique experience of God. What's more, that soccer fan—in one class session—is already a qualified evangelist: he can connect the ineffable divine clearly with his daily life, and explain how the church celebrates that experience in worship. Wells' use of two simple words has amazing implications for the way Christians minister in the world, and endless potential for enlivening the church with each new visitor.

Throwing Away the Oars. *Kristin Berkey-Abbott*

I've been thinking about those ancient Celtic monks who set off in coracles, sometimes without even an oar, to see where God would lead them. I've been thinking about the Feast of Transfiguration and the Feast of Annunciation, Feast days that bookend the Feast Day of St. Patrick, and thinking about all the ways that God has transformed history, often by leading people who weren't always sure where they were going. I've been thinking about mainline churches and the stories we hear of decline. I've been thinking about aging church buildings and aging parishioners. I've been wondering what God will do next.

I know that some churches have responded to recent changes by trying to update their worship experience: maybe a rock band, maybe get rid of the pews, maybe have a self-help focus to the sermons. I know that many more are clinging ever more tightly to what we've always done, at least for the past century or so. But what would happen if we threw away those oars?

What would church look like if we didn't already think we knew what church should look like?

Would we take advantage of this depressed real estate market to create a different sort of Christian community? Would we get rid of property altogether and set out to see the world and see where God led us? Would we return to ancient creative arts or forge something new with modern technology?

What wild areas would we cultivate?

Check out more of Kristin's work at liberationtheologhlutheran.blogspot.com *or at* kristinberkey-abbott.com

The Musical Score Comes from God.
Roger Hungerford

Roger wrote in response to our question "We've chosen a boat without oars as the metaphor for the future of the church. What metaphor do you think best describes the church as it discerns and works toward a vital and bold expression in the 21st Century?"

While I like the metaphor of a boat without oars, where God is the primary motive and directive force, the metaphor that I continue to embrace for the church, even as the church is experiencing a transfiguration, is a musical group. For me, this resonates because making music is a synergistic effort. Anyone who has created an original piece of art knows that the source of the inspiration is beyond him or her. Art is truly divine communication (yes even what some would consider bad art is a unique way of expressing God). The same is true with musical compositions. The score comes from God. It is then interpreted and expressed by humans in a variety of different ways from large orchestras performing a complexly organized piece in an ornate concert hall to one person singing *a capella* on a street corner. Additionally, within the wonder of music are the awesome array of instruments and the wondrous diversity of musical genres. The same can be said of the church. We have a vast array of interpretation and expression, along with an awesome collection of instruments and a wondrous diversity. All of this is our way of joining our voices with angels and archangels and all the company of heaven participating in praise of God. What we are seeing now is the search for new ways of sharing of expression—possibly the creation of new instruments, definitely the creation of a new form of music. I think that the Church's acknowledged or unacknowledged discerning of "a vital and bold expression in the 21st Century" will ultimately be a synergistic complement to our existing Church.

Roger Hungerford is now the Vicar of All Saints Episcopal Church in Moline, Illinois, where he lives with his wife Liz. He received his Master of Divinity at the Seminary of the Southwest in Austin, Texas.

Questions

What does "evangelism" mean to you?

What creates the discomfort many Christians feel regarding evangelism?

What role does evangelism play in the future of the church?

When it comes to evangelism, whose story are we telling? Ours? Our community's? God's?

How do you connect worship with your workweek? How would you answer Wells' four questions? (from *Incense and Soccer Balls*)

About wild geese:

The artwork pasted behind the "Question" pages features wild geese. Wild geese are an ancient Celtic symbol for the Holy Spirit. Describing this, one New Zealand pastor writes:

> The wild goose is one of the most communal of creatures, drawing its life from the flock. God's Spirit is not a spirit of individualism, but of community. In an age when the spirit of individualism is a supreme ideology both outside and inside the church, it is worth reminding ourselves that the testimony of the earliest Christians, and of Christians down the ages, is that the Spirit brings community. That was a primary message of the Pentecost narrative. The Spirit, when it is *holy* Spirit, brings people together, to support and travel life's journey with each other.[8]

---

[8] David Clark, "The Celtic Wild Goose is a Great Symbol for the Holy Spirit and for St. Luke's." May 31, 2009, www.stluke.org.nz/?sid=42258.

APRIL 2012: GATHERING PROVISIONS

The word "mercurial" came to mind this April in Austin. The skies offered soaring temperatures, strong winds, a chill, and much-needed rain before a probable predictably dry summer. Observing the church calendar, we had a long Lenten season waiting for the arrival of a "late" Easter. In our own home, we faced the end of the school year and final exams. Like other seminary families, we weathered the tension that arose when students stayed up late and left more often to find a quiet place to study. This mercurial month had us drawing on stored resources and preparing for a new season: Easter, summer, freedom.

For *Boats without Oars*, April meant gathering supplies and making provisions for the journey: reservations made, more grants requested, juggling final exams and long e-mail lists of potential participants for our study, final doctors' appointments for the children, new tires for the car, grieving the sudden loss of a dear family pet, final meetings with spiritual directors. The traffic on the *Boats without Oars* blog increased dramatically; guest bloggers approached "evangelism" from many interesting angles. We spent more time doing our own research and writing (and preaching in Michael's case.) This was a month full of possibility, transition, and waiting. By the last few weeks of April, we were excited to get out on the open road.

—Kristin

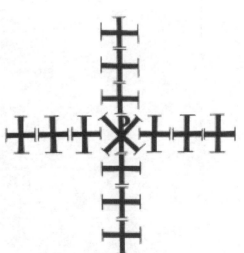

The symbol of "Jesus Sending Forth the Twelve" was drawn by Rudolf Koch (1876-1934) and is available on the public domain.

Planting Seeds. *Kristin*

This evening, our family gathered around a small glass jar and mixed soil with ashes and buried wheat berries beneath the humus, then doused the mixture with water and processed around the yard then through the corridors of our house singing a song about Jesus entering Jerusalem riding on a donkey, preparing himself to die so that we may live. With good care and a bit of luck, the seeds will sprout by Easter morning, a visible sign of the necessary death of the seeds to bring life. It is Palm Sunday, the beginning of Holy Week, a season within the season of Lent, to prepare us to celebrate the life that is to come on Easter.

Planting seeds is an act of faith that continues to bring wonder and joy to our children (and even to us adults when we pause to contemplate the wonderful miracle of death transforming to life). I see other types of seeds planted all around me during this time of year. The Texan flora and fauna are exploding with life after the deadly drought of last year. Parents of young children all around us faithfully and diligently continue to guide their children into abundant life through the hard work of discipline and humility, and then watch their children blossom after seasons of temper tantrums and frustration, again and again. All of the prayers and petitions of my grandparents on my behalf throughout the years are a blanket of seeds I wear as a daily cloak. Hours spent listening to lectures, studying, writing, and practicing produce new ideas and fabulous papers and sermons by the seminarians all around me here at the Seminary. And, most poignantly to me this week, a student knocked on my door and handed me a check as a donation toward *Boats without Oars* to help us launch our mission. She handed me the first donation of our mission in great faith, planting a seed, anticipating the sweet and rich fruit that will come.

As church, where do we collectively plant seeds? Some individuals practice stewardship by planting time, treasure, and talent into their church communities. Groups pool resources together and make sure children at the local school have some food to take home in their backpacks each day or that medical care is available at a church sponsored free clinic. Maybe churches combine efforts and transform an entire city, county, state, nation, and the world. However, seeds are tiny and sometimes we feel our resources are tiny. Sometimes it feels like a bit of a death for us to plant ourselves into a difficult relationship, to authentically be with someone, or to delay or forgo making a financial purchase so that we may plant our resources instead into a community initiative.

Let us not forget that with faith, time, and miracle, death transforms to life, that everything we need to live is within our grasp. Jesus said, "I tell you the truth, unless a kernel of wheat is planted in the soil and dies, it remains alone. But its death will produce many new kernels—a plentiful harvest of new lives" (John 12:24, NLT).

Our Children, the Outsiders. *Michael*

A priest recently Tweeted the phrase "parents should be just as devoted to the spiritual formation of their children as they are to driving them to soccer practice." This was one of several things he broadcast that day, mostly fun little comments about the Christian life, but this one made me think. Tending the spirituality of my children often perplexes me: I want them to encounter our faith in ways they find meaningful, AND I want them honored as brothers and sisters in the church. The Episcopal Church certainly has fantastic resources for children's formation, but I sense a deep disconnect when it comes to incorporating children in weekly worship. I've talked with many priests about including children in Sunday services, and the consensus is that to do it well, the leader has to be incredibly innovative and charismatic (in other words: "not us"). While tending the souls of children can seem daunting, what could be more worthwhile? Children's worship and spirituality is a topic very much worth exploring.

If evangelism is all about proclaiming the gospel (and we are charged both in the Bible and in our baptismal vows to do so), clearly we need to spend some energy as a church learning how to better transmit the gospel to the upcoming generations. I've been contemplating this lately. I think children are in some ways the ultimate archetype of the community outsider: they smell funny, they worship in ways that make most Episcopalians flinch uncomfortably, they are loud, and they don't obey the rules. But the thing is, they are also **us**. We eat with them daily, talk with them (endlessly, it sometimes seems!), and share our space and our time with them generously; they are in communion with us in almost every sense of the word. Yet, somehow, our worship and prayer often separate us in profound ways: they become outsiders in their own community. My conclusion: until we can incorporate *these* particular outsiders—the ones that *are* us—we won't be able to truly welcome people from outside the church walls.

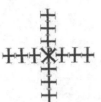

The Calling Cross. *Kristin*

Last night, the Seminary of the Southwest community gathered to celebrate one of the most ancient rituals in the Christian church, the Great Holy Vigil of Easter. The symbols and movements were primitive: a group of black-robed priests lighting an outdoor fire and saying prayers, the light of Christ embodied in a candle lit by the bon fire, the hoard of people following the light into the chapel. Inside we sang and chanted the ancient Psalms in darkness, waiting for the sanctuary to be brought to life. Then, in a great force of energy, Jesus figuratively bursts forth from the tomb, breaking the bonds of injustice; the lights raise, candles extinguish, bells ring, cheering, singing, great vases of flowers placed all around us. We baptized babies, got showered with water from the life-giving font, flung out over us by green branches, took Communion, sang jubilantly, then we were streaming outside the chapel doors to go celebrate together in the dining hall with cakes and fruit, and punch and champagne.

Symbols surrounded us: students ignited the Holy fire outside in the courtyard to remind us that Jesus returned to the world. Shadows on limestone walls shifted from dark to light inside the chapel, designed in the shape of a Bedouin tent to remind us that we are all just travelers passing through. In the fading evening light, we looked out the clear glass windows to the cross that stands outside of Christ Chapel. This symbol reminds us that the work of the church is out in the world. I have often heard this particular cross referred to as the "Calling Cross," and its imagery is one of the reasons Michael and I chose to come live in this particular seminary community.

We worshippers walked into the chapel doors following the light, the light burst forth upon us, we celebrated, and then we departed to go out into the world to do the work that God has called us to do. We are on mission; we are evangelizing.

Jesus left the tomb to be out in the world, once again walking on the streets with his friends, teaching, sharing meals, singing, celebrating. Jesus was no stranger to the temple. In fact, his first public appearance after being tested in the wilderness was to enter a synagogue to teach (Luke 4:16-21). But he didn't stay there; he's always on the move, searching for those who need some attention, some healing, some stories, some life.

A few years ago, while living in the Diocese of Olympia, we studied Bishop Greg Rickel's book selection for Lent: *Missional Renaissance* by author Reggie McNeal. One of my favorite metaphors from the book was that church should be more like an airport—a place one is glad to be in for the needs it provides, but a place not luxurious enough to tarry for long—always a place of departure. I think our churches' liturgies and our evangelizing, at their best, honor that idea: we prepare, we gather, we worship, we nourish, we go out into the world.

The "Calling Cross" outside the Seminary of the Southwest chapel, Austin, Texas. Public Domain.

Preaching Evangelism. *Michael*

I've been writing and reading about evangelism, about the story we tell about our faith.[9] This Easter, the passage Matthew 28:9-15, the first resurrection appearance of Jesus, appears in the Lectionary. Looking ahead to a hopefully long career, I'm more than a little interested in where the church is going, and I think a lot of it has to do with how we tell the story right now. There are dueling narratives:

From one group of voices we have "mainline decline," or—even better—there's that strange solace we take lately in knowing that everybody [all American churches, that is] is shrinking now, it's not just us anymore. We have the story of a once-proud heritage that has become largely irrelevant to culture that surrounds us. We are closing ranks and turning inward: keeping alive a set of traditions that will only further alienate us from the world around us. The only trick is just to rip the Band-aid off: get rid of that staid morose insistence on a particular type of morality or theology or vision of church. Make it exciting. Get a drum set, for God's sake!

And then there's the other story: It's the "fortuitous moment" for ritual and liturgical traditions who have a meaningful and rich connection with the ancient church and the spirituality of a different world. We have the benefit of a firm commitment to ask the difficult questions and wrestle with ambiguity. It's the time of ragtag gatherings of half-hopeful, half-confused wannabe believers who know they are spiritual beings and that Jesus has for them something beyond the "as seen on TV" faith they've been exposed to. It's the story of resurgence amidst slipping budgets and declining membership. It's a call to go back to Galilee, that is: to the Galilee of the best of Jesus' ministry of everyday living and healing the sick and casting out the demons and—most of all—spreading the Good News of the Kingdom of God. Go back, because the Lord who you seek is not here in the tomb.

For the guards who take their unbelievable and terrifying story back to the chief priests, there is little to look forward to. They saw, with their own eyes, the earth-rending fiery light of the greatest reversal of all time, and instead chose to say that they were asleep. And they will be. They are willfully blind, dead to the

---

[9] This text is from a sermon Michael preached during Easter 2012 at Christ Chapel, Seminary of the Southwest in Austin, Texas.

possibilities of new life, all for the sake of a comfortable living and keeping out of trouble with their superiors. Theirs is a story of an empty tomb, but because of deception: they would have us believe that the disciples of Jesus simply propagated a story for their own prestige, working only to add followers to their movement and give a little extra jolt to next year's capital campaign.

The two Marys, though, come telling the truth. It is equally unbelievable. The resurrection, if it is to be believed, means that death and cynicism no longer have the last word. It means that hope will not die, even though it be crushed again and again under the wheels of an uncaring world. They have Good News—they are evangelizing—and their work is cut out for them. They have a future story that turns the present world on its head.

So when we tell the story of the future of the church, whose story are we telling? Do we keep our heads down, stay up all night and succumb to the stress of an endless set of expectations? Given that, wouldn't you take the bribe: tell the folks the story they want to hear just so you can get some peace and quiet? Or do we break out of convention just a bit? Introduce a new perspective? Find new ways to tell the world that there really is resurrection? Jesus said, "Do not be afraid; go and tell my brothers to go to Galilee; there they will see me" (Matt. 28.10, NIV).

Fear and Evangelism. *Kristin*

"Action is one of the best remedies for fear." I taped this simple quote taken from a magazine article to my closet door as a daily reminder to walk outside and embrace life, resist the urge to stay inside my "safe" house, and remember to meet the gaze of a stranger. The words ask me to welcome strangers as fellow human beings, with all the accompanying joys and struggles that greet each of us during our earthly existence.

That magazine quotation seems like an ideal in a culture that likes to bombard me with shocking stories of separation, mayhem, violence, an increasing escalation of doubt and fear. Being a parent intensifies this discomfort. I feel discord between Jesus telling me to "love your neighbor as yourself" and the confusion and fear I feel about how to engage "strangers" in our neighborhood park. There I may find a Latino woman pushing an Anglo child in a stroller, a dark-hooded man hunched over and sleeping on the nearby picnic table, or a college kid walking briskly by, eyes to the ground. Why am I afraid of these people?

In *Free Range Kids: Giving Our Children the Freedom We Had without Going Nuts with Worry,* author Lenore Skenazy does a masterful job of debunking many beliefs that seem to be at the root of some common parenting fears. She provides thoughtful and practical analysis and advice on how to let our children live more fully in our world instead of spending an increasing amount of time in cars and behind closed doors and writes that, "Millions of [parents] now see the world so fraught with danger that they can't possibly let their children explore it" (p. 5). Skenazy relates many stories from countries other than the United States, where children spend hours playing at neighborhood playgrounds with no parental supervision. Can you imagine? In fact, parents in many other countries "just seem to trust their children and their fellow citizens more" (p. 86). Why?

Many factors seem to contribute to this general distrust of our neighbors, from fear of lawsuits, to fear of being blamed and labeled as "bad" or "untrustworthy" by peers, to media focus on shocking but rare crimes.

What does it mean to evangelize—or even be hospitable—in what many call a "culture of fear?"

One response to this troubling but necessary question comes from Dr. Scott Bader-Saye, the Seminary of the Southwest's Professor of Christian Ethics and Moral Theology. In his 2009 book *Following Jesus in a Culture of Fear*. He writes,

> Following Jesus will mean surrendering the power that masquerades as security in order to love the neighbor and welcome the stranger. It will mean avoiding the safe path in order to pursue the good. But in a culture of fear, we find such risks all the more difficult, since our natural inclinations lead us to close in on ourselves when we face danger. How can we maintain the posture of the open hand toward a world that scares us (p. 22)?

Bader-Saye challenges individuals as well as communities where people sometimes cloister to the exclusion of the broader world. Quoting sociologist Zygmunt Bauman,

> Out there, in the street, all sorts of dangers lie in ambush; we have to be alert when we go out, watch whom we are talking to and who talks to us, be on the lookout every minute. In here in the community, we can relax—we are safe, there are no dangers looming in dark corners. But in this "elusive paradise" there is a "price to be paid, and that price includes the diminishing or extinguishing of hospitality" (p. 104).

Here I am again, back to this conundrum of wondering how to be a bearer of Good News when I am literally afraid of the stranger I pass on my daily walk to the coffee shop or the playground or in the grocery checkout line. I'm not even talking about having a conversation where the name or notion of "God" is inserted; I'm often not even getting to "hello!" I know I am not alone in this quandary and that often our own Christian church communities are just as blinded, muted, and shuffling along, not knowing how, or if, to trust those other "strangers" we pass on our sidewalks.

Bader-Saye provides some guidance on how to be more hospitable to the stranger by reminding us to look back to the ancient communities, those living in the few hundred years after the death of Jesus. The first Christian communities were clearly Jewish, but with Jesus' command to go love, and to share the Good News of his Kingdom to *all* people, the boundaries of that community began to be challenged. The apostle Philip baptizes the Ethiopian, Peter breaks Jewish law by lodging and eating with a Roman centurion, Paul and Barnabas receive hospitality from the Gentiles.

> This experience in the life of the church gives Christians today a window into the radical hospitality that was necessary for the church to live into its calling in its earliest days. Welcoming the Gentiles was a risky move on all counts, but the willingness of the church to take such a risk provides a paradigm of hospitality for the church today as we face our own temptations to draw sharp boundaries and keep ourselves safe from a hostile world (p. 107).

I'm still working this out, looking at that quote on my closet door, and remembering that moving toward being hospitable and evangelical may start with an action as simple as making eye contact, deeply listening, giving a hug, trusting. Most of all, I will have to work on believing some ancient truths—that God created the world and called it "good"—and created humans and called them "very good" and that Jesus said, "the thief comes only to steal and kill and destroy. I came that they may have life, and have it abundantly" (John 10:10). I want to keep working on choosing that abundant life—sharing the abundance of my own life wherever I land—and not believing the lies and falling prey to the cultural thieves, beliefs, and fears that want to rob me of the joy of living in this good world with very, very good people.

"To love wastefully and give recklessly—that scares us,"[10] writes Reverend Lynice Pinkard. She's absolutely right, and she's speaking to me, and to all of us about living out Jesus' terrifying proclamations to "love our enemies," "sell everything you have and give it to the poor," or "pray for those who persecute you." We stand mute in the grocery store line, stare uncomfortably ahead and turn up our car stereo next to the man holding a cardboard sign asking for money next to the interstate on-ramp. What does evangelizing mean and how will we follow Jesus' command to go to *all* people and share the Good News when we live in such a state of fear?

---

[10] Mark Leviton. "Dangerous Love: Reverend Lynice Pinkard on the Revolutionary Act of Living the Gospels," *The Sun*, October 2014, p. 9.

Faced with overwhelm that leads to ambivalence, it seems easier to keep our doors locked and draw the reigns in tighter around our children and ourselves. However, Reverend Pinkard encourages us:

> But our goal is progress, not perfection. If we can't love our enemies, we can start by loving the people who love us back and then move on from there to people we find a little suspect, and then to the people we don't like at all. Resurrection and salvation are about the kind of love that overcomes our own self-interest. If I'm interacting with the world primarily as an investment and looking to make a good return, I'm losing my life. Real relationships aren't investments. Community is not a contract; it's a covenant.[11]

Photo Credit: Kristin Carroccino. Bravely Opening the Door. Dinosaur National Monument, Utah. 2010.

---

[11] ibid.

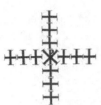

21st Century Church. *Michael*

In the spring of 2012, I attended a series of lectures given by Presiding Bishop Katherine Jefferts-Schori entitled "Being the Church in the 21st Century." Her fast-paced presentation traversed a broad range of topics: polity, worship, evangelism, mission, spiritual practice, clergy roles, ecclesiology, and more. Based on what she has seen her travels around the Episcopal Church, she approached each subject as a facet of her overall vision of the church's future.

Throughout the lectures, an icon of "Rublev's *Trinity*" served as the guiding image. According to Schori, the Trinity is an eternal *conversation*: not in a contemporary sense of the word, but in an archaic usage with implications of ongoing communion and relationship. She related this nuanced sense of conversation to the theological term *perichoresis*: the "eternal dance" or "mutual indwelling" of the Trinity. As God's church, our work is to incarnate this Trinitarian Conversation in the world.

Evangelism

Starting with evangelism, Bishop Schori explored the implications of this guiding image. The essence of her evangelism is hospitality, but—again—not in the everyday sense. More than simply hosting or providing for another, she broadens hospitality to include our readiness to accept gifts from others. Through this lens, evangelism becomes a practice of looking for and identifying the gifts we see in others, and encouraging them to use those gifts in conversation with the Trinity. Instead of analytic scrutiny, Schori wishes the Trinity inspired our churches more toward conversation. The Trinity is a divine mystery best entered in community, and the hospitable conversation of evangelism prepares us to learn from one another as we walk the journey.

Leadership

Jefferts-Schori next extended her Trinitarian vision to church leadership. Leaders, she said, must be agents of change: our goal is the Kingdom of God, and we clearly aren't there yet! Thus change is inevitable, and leaders must prepare for it. Schori described leadership as complex, dynamic, and shared. She detailed a list of identifying markers for effective change agents:

Kenotic leaders will not hold on to power or self-interest, preferring instead to empty themselves of the gifts they have to share.

Collaborative leadership implies a kind of solidarity with those who are different and a shared interest and ownership in the common good.

† **Courageous** leaders must be willing to fail in pursuit of a good end. The Bishop used the metaphor of mountaineers, who must evaluate both the subjective (perceived) risks and objective (actual) risks of a venture realistically before making sound decisions.

† **Grounded** leaders must have as their center a strong connection to the "deep well" of our own self-awareness and spiritual practice; and also cultivate relationships with peers who are not afraid to tell the truths we don't want to hear. "Spirituality," she said, "is the fundamental willingness to face what is real."

† **Curious** leaders must have a thirst for exploration, a willingness to wander in the wilderness and climb the hills that no one has ever climbed before, and they must be willing to look with fresh eyes at the world around them in order to create a healthy space for discernment.

† **Creative** leaders think outside of the box, "which in some cases has become a grave."

† **Humble** leadership includes a willingness to travel light, to be low maintenance, and to receive the gifts that others have to offer.

† **Formed in the Vision of the Common Good,** leaders will resist the cultural mode of sorting all conflict into a binary of winners and losers. This means that leaders must cultivate communal values, share their power, and create a culture of abundance—the resources are there to give all what they need to thrive.

Schori says the work of identifying quality leaders is to keep our eyes open for people displaying these characteristics, and then do our best to get out of their way.

Local Church, Global Church

In a highly nuanced critique of Episcopal Church polity, the Presiding Bishop noted that democracy has varied models. Our deliberative/legislative model creates sharply divided categories of winners and losers by encouraging the formation of power dynamics and interest groups. We strive to build consensus but often succumb to competition and infighting. Bishop Schori prefers the model of a commonweal: rather than legislation, we need conversation; a communal discernment that seeks the good of the whole.

Jefferts-Schori's hopes the church will be a prophetic model of holy living to the world around us, and she used the Episcopal Church's "Five Marks of Mission" to clarify this goal: [12]

† To proclaim the Good News of the Kingdom.
† To teach, baptize, and nurture new believers.
† To respond to human need by loving service.
† To seek to transform unjust structures of society, to challenge violence of every kind, and to pursue peace and reconciliation.
† To strive to safeguard the integrity of creation and sustain and renew the life of the earth.

By modeling Christian community on these five marks, and by seeking partners in that work, Bishop Schori feels we can work together to address global issues like just economy and governance, peacemaking, reconciliation. We will become a people who eschew our culture's radical individualism in favor of interdependence. Incarnating this kind of Christian community requires binary vision: our awareness must encompass both the local and the global implications of what we do. At every level, our mission insists that we work together to create a shared vision of the common good that reflects the Kingdom of God. Abandonment, infighting, and power struggles serve only to sever the local from the global, leaving communities unable to share in the whole of God's redemptive work. If we are to live out our mission with integrity, it requires of us that basic Trinitarian activity: we have to keep the conversation going.

---

[12] "The Five Marks of Mission," http://www.episcopalchurch.org/page/five-marks-mission.

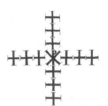

Creeds. *Kristin*

"The Glory of God is the human person fully alive; and life consists in beholding God."
—St. Irenaeus, 2nd Century

In an adult formation class this morning at St. David's Episcopal Church in Austin, I was reminded that we Episcopalians are people of practice. When one asks, "what do Episcopalians believe?" the answer is found by looking at what Episcopalians profess in their creeds and covenants, not so much about what the individual parishioner believes about a particular verse in the Bible or political ideology of the day. Now, on any given day, I, individually, may have trouble agreeing with every phrase in all of the Prayer Book creeds, but the operative language and beauty in sharing these texts communally, is that, for the most part, the phrases begin with "we," and I can trust that the church universal is affirming my Christian belief when I doubt. This is Good News.

My teacher this morning, Amy Moehnke, the Young Adults Ministry Coordinator at St. David's, skillfully challenged our group to examine how closely the practices of our daily lives match what we profess we believe by reflecting on the Baptismal Covenant from the *Book of Common Prayer*, a set of statements many of us have heartily repeated at baptisms or confirmations. Near the end of these statements proclaiming what we believe, is a query that speaks to our evangelical duty:

Celebrant   Will you proclaim by word and example the Good News of God in Christ?

People   I will, with God's help.

So then, how do the practices of my life reflect what I state I believe, that I will proclaim the Good News of Christ with God's help? What is the Good News I am going to proclaim? I think the ancient theologian Irenaeus captures the essence of our relationship to God and what God wants most for humanity: to live in full knowledge of the love, power, and mystery of God and to work toward reconciling the world back to the knowledge of this love. That looks like being fully alive, completely full of the essence of who I was created to be, and thus continuously beholding God in my life. I think that is very Good, albeit really challenging, News.

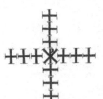

The Art of Seeing God. *Michael*

Here we are in Easter 2: Low Sunday.[13] We still have 42 more days of Easter, but how much staying power does Easter have for us, really? What makes it real to us? How on Earth can we explain why something is so great that we spend such a big chunk of every year observing it officially in the church?

Let's review a section of today's reading from 1 John:

> We declare to you what was from the beginning, what we have heard, what we have seen with our eyes, what we have looked at and touched with our hands, concerning the word of life…we declare to you what we have seen and heard so that you also may have fellowship with us; and truly our fellowship is with the Father and with his Son Jesus Christ. We are writing these things so that our joy may be complete (1 John 1: 1-4, NRSV).

When I read this, the words I notice are communicating words: heard, seen, touched; we declare. And notice why they declare: "so that you may have fellowship with us," and "so that our joy may be complete." The people who wrote these books felt the Gospel as a burning call in their lives: they had seen and heard and even touched the savior of the world, and they knew something that they could not contain. Jesus was a real and abiding presence in their lives, and they couldn't help but talk about him.

Our faith seems to have a bit of an emphasis on talking, on words, on breath. Even back at the beginning, God spoke it into existence, God made humans from the dust and breathed life into them. In John's gospel today, Jesus spoke words of sending and of peace. He breathed on them. It's almost as if some part of the truth of God's story happens simply in telling it. After all—that's what we gather here together for every Sunday, right? We tell the story, and tell it, and tell it— week after week. And we believe that when we tell it, we live it. When the priest

---

[13] This is a sermon for the Second Sunday in Easter, traditionally called "Low Sunday'. The readings for the day include John 20:19-31 and 1 John 1:1 - 2:2. The idea of evangelism as the "Art of Seeing God" really became paradigmatic for *Boats without Oars*, and I (Michael) was glad for the opportunity to work out some of my ideas in public. I preached this sermon at St. Michael's and All Angels in Austin, Texas.

calls the Holy Spirit to come and sanctify the bread and wine, to come a sanctify US, we experience that same breath of God again. Now, most weeks it certainly doesn't FEEL like that's what's going on, but I don't think God's work can be held up too much by my feelings! So it is for our own words: when we speak God's story, we live it; and when we're telling God's story, when we bring it to life for all the world to see—that's Easter, that's resurrection.

And what is that story? What makes it so worth telling? Look what John says here:

> "This is the message we have heard from him and proclaim to
> you, that God is light and in him there is no darkness at all"
> (1 John 1:5, ESV).

Those are some profound words—there is NO darkness AT ALL. I could preach an entire sermon on that. But there's trouble here in that I hear these kinds of sentiments so often that they lose their power, they have little meaning for me. The problem, I think, is that I hear them: I don't retell them. I don't come up with my own words for them. I don't bring them to life. That's the trick: if, like John, we want our joy to be complete, we have to declare and proclaim these same healing words in our own lives and to the people we love. We have to evangelize.

Now, I don't want you to hear what I'm NOT saying: the point of this sermon is not to get you to go stand on a street corner with a bullhorn and tell everybody about Jesus (only a few people are called to that, and most of them are already doing it!). Notice with me that two times in the Gospel today, the disciples are gathered behind closed doors. Jesus doesn't come in with the guilt trip "Hey, why aren't you out there telling the world about me?" No: he speaks words of peace and love. He affirms them in what they are already doing. I think these are some comforting stories for the church: no matter how well we lock the doors, Jesus gets in any way! So the proclamation comes later, it comes after the disciples have really experienced the risen Lord in such measure that they just can't keep their mouths shut.

Evangelism, as in the experience of the disciples, is a natural part of a life lived in the Spirit. Let me unpack that a little: I've been studying evangelism quite a bit lately, and my definition is quickly evolving. When I say evangelism, I don't mean the heavy pressure of always having the right words to say or of feeling like it's your responsibility to save the soul of every stranger you meet. Soul-saving is certainly at the heart of evangelism—it's at the heart of all God's work—but we have to remember that it's not us who are doing the saving. I think evangelism is about finding a language that faithfully expresses our experience of God and recognizes the experiences of others. The author of 1 John tells us that he is proclaiming a gospel that was from the beginning of the world, so we have to think that if we're in that world, we're already surrounded by that gospel and we just have to learn how to see it.

I have a friend who is a graphic designer, and he told me once that learning to draw was not so much about learning how to use a pen and paper, but about learning how to see things in such a way that you could bring out the most significant parts in your art. So it is with spirituality: we are immersed in a world of deep and profound truth, and our words become the way by which we recreate the most significant parts of it. We should listen to how we talk: I think it is in how we tell our stories, how we tell the church's story, and how we tell the world's story that we discover how we truly live. If we believe prayer really changes things, how does it? If there truly is hope for the world, what does that look like when you're stuck in 5 o'clock traffic 20 days a month? If your friend at work seems to always display a peace that passes understanding, do you have the words to recognize the beauty of that with her and celebrate it together?

If you find you don't have the words for that kind of talk just yet: don't despair. Be like Thomas: look your God straight in the eye and give him a good jab in the ribs before you're ready to announce the good news. It's OK, God can take it. In the story today, Jesus came through a locked door to reach the faithful skeptic. Sometimes faith takes time to work itself out; sometimes the things we say in our worship are unbelievable. But we keep showing up, we keep telling the story, and—amazingly—we keep seeing it lived out in the most unexpected ways. Our job as evangelists is not to be cheerleaders for God, always making our faith look good so other folks will be attracted to it. Our job as evangelists is to learn to see God all around us in the world God created and sustains, and to name the beauty and hope and joy of God for what they are. God and faith are very real parts of our lives, as real as the bread and the wine on the altar, and God has faith in the power of our words to tell out that peace and joy that he sent out with the disciples in that very first week of Easter.

So, as you go about your work this week, or you sit down with your kids, or as you share a meal with a stranger, or as you hang out with your friends: don't expend your energy trying to WORK God into the conversation. Instead, focus just a little bit of extra attention on trying to FIND God in the conversation, because this is God's world, after all, and God is already there. In so doing, we act out our parts as the priesthood of all believers, or as my liturgy professor likes to say: the priesthood of the cosmos. We become the guides, the signposts that mark God's activity in a world where it is largely obscured. We remind the world of its origin in a God that is all light, a God who has no darkness whatsoever. We breathe out the Holy Spirit to people who desperately want her peace. Now that's Easter, that's something worth celebrating for a few extra days.

Photo credit: Kristin Carroccino. Standing in the Light. Burr Trail, Utah. August 2012.

Outfitting for the Journey. *Kristin*

Sail forth! Seer for the deep waters only!
Reckless, O soul, exploring, I with thee, and thou with me;
For we are bound where mariner has not yet dared to go,
And we will risk the ship, ourselves and all.
O my brave soul!
O farther, farther sail!
O daring joy, but safe! Are they not all the seas of God?
O farther, farther, farther sail!
—From Walt Whitman's "Passage to India"

In less than two weeks, we depart on our summer voyage, a journey across the United States in pursuit of meeting Episcopal leaders and churches and sharing the stories of those who are embracing and living into the changing reality of church in the 21st Century. In between collecting church narratives, we will also have some family vacation time, camping and visiting extended family. This is a big expedition, and I have been spending a lot of time creating packing lists, and to-do lists of what needs to happen before we launch the Toyota Camry away from Austin with two adults and two young children. I'm outfitting our lives and our vessel; we are preparing for adventure.

Our lists include things like oil changes, and car organizers, systems of food distribution, campground reservation printouts, bedding, books, art supplies, arranging for neighbors to tend to our share in the community chicken cooperative. Will we sublet our house? What will we eat? Can we really afford this?!

As a church, what would outfitting for mission in the 21st Century include? If the missional church launched on a boat without oars, what would it need to fare well on the journey? To thrive where the Spirit of God lands the boat?

Here are some thoughts:

1) **A supporting community**: These are the individuals who are on the shore ready to launch the boat: the praying elders, the administrative leaders, the generous financiers, the bakers of bread for the journey, the builders of the boat, and the ones who may remain behind occasionally wringing their hands in worry, waiting to hear news from abroad and alternately lifting hands in praise to God for the success of the mission.

2) **The men and women in the boats**: With a fierce sense of call and deep compassion and energy for the unknown that lies ahead, they have spent much time in prayer and discernment and are ready to step in and be launched into the vast expanse. They are vulnerable, and they must learn to be transparent and authentic in their interactions.

3) **The water**: The vast depths will both gently, and sometimes violently, carry the boat and passengers along. This is the great connector from the secure land behind and the mysterious territory just beyond the horizon.

4) **The people on the other side**: The community and the passengers are setting off in faith that new friends in the unknown land will greet them, that there will be needs there that can be tended to with all of the love and compassion that the people in the homeland have cultivated for so many years. The passengers are the messengers. They bring Good News.

In the end, sometimes we can get caught up in a lot of details: how many pairs of shorts, spare shoes, how thick of a sweater, how many copies of *The Book of Common Prayer*, how many hours spent in committees, what kind of cookies do we need for coffee hour, or which font should the administrative assistant use in the bulletins? But what's necessary to bring about transformation, whether personal or corporate, is a loving community that looks clearly at the risks and conflicts that lay ahead and supports those who venture out or toil within, open hearts, means of transport, and trust that we are being faithful to the adventure that is the movement of God.

"Imagination is more important than knowledge. For knowledge is limited to all we now know and understand, while imagination embraces the entire world, and all there ever will be to know and understand."
—Albert Einstein

"Why Church?" *Jonathan Weldon*

Father Jonathan Weldon, of St. Paul's Episcopal Church in Bellingham, Washington, wrote in response to our question, "Why church?"

The Church is composed of people assembled by the Holy Spirit to receive the Good News, seek to be formed and shaped by it, and to communicate that Good News to others in a way that calls them into the community where the Gospel can be heard and taught.

St. Paul's has to offer our community a very visible presence by virtue of our building, and a life of worship shaped by historic liturgical patterns in which the Scriptures of both testaments are read and heard and the sacraments which communicate the essence of the Good News are shared weekly. For our children, we have Godly Play, a way for children to listen and hear that Good News that engages their imagination.

Photo from St. Paul's Episcopal Church, Bellingham, Washington, website: www.stpaulsbellingham.org.

Inspired by the example of Phinney Ridge Lutheran Church's (Seattle) catechumenal process called "The Way" as experienced in their weekend called "Faith and Font," we are in the process of developing an adult catechumenate in order to facilitate a process to engage the imaginations of participants in receiving and embodying the Good News. The aim is to create a different context in which to be church; a context of shared conversation and fellowship in which the already-baptized and those seeking baptism grow in understanding as they encounter the Scriptures and the sacraments that mediate God's love for the world. I expect that as this practice develops there will be many people who are made evangelists by virtue of being able to say they belong to a meaningful community that engenders faith in a gracious and good God.

St. Paul's also offers public witness to the values of the Gospel by our ministry of meeting people in temporal need through a weekly invitation to share with groups of parishioners those needs and receive tangible help and comfort.

St. Paul's also has stewardship of buildings and a congregation that together represent resources for the development of new forms of ministry to bless the community in the name of Christ, and we are actively seeking to realize and embark upon these new forms of ministry.

Jonathan Weldon serves as rector of St. Paul's Episcopal Church in Bellingham, Washington, having previously served congregations in Oregon and in the office of a Bishop. With his wife Sharon, he is the proud parent of two daughters in their twenties.

What Evangelism Means to Me.
Mary Balfour Van Zandt

It is an honor to support my friends Kristin and Michael on their journey to seek how we can build God's Kingdom. I must admit that the word evangelism is not a word I have been comfortable with in the past. As an Episcopalian, I have always had the mindset that evangelism meant going to foreign countries and putting Bible's in peoples' hands or standing on a street corner and professing the power of God. I know, I know!—a total misconception of the word!!!

Since I have been in seminary, I have realized that evangelism is necessary to build God's Kingdom. It also doesn't have to be done in the ways that I conceived. Evangelism can include hospitality, taking someone a meal that is ill, sitting and listening, spreading the Good News of God's love. In the end, isn't evangelism what God calls us all to do? It sure feels that way to me. I now understand the word evangelism to mean to plant seeds of God's amazing love for us.

I want to thank Kristin and Michael for being brave enough to use this word and to explore its true meaning. To ask people the question, what is evangelism and what does it mean to you? How can we bring our brothers and sisters in to the Kingdom of God? I think Kristin and Michael are doing just that. Blessings to you my friends on your journey, may we all be so brave and learn from you.

Mary Balfour Van Zandt is now the Deacon in Charge at St. Michael's Episcopal Church in Fayette, Alabama, and is a graduate of the Seminary of the Southwest. Mary Balfour loves walking her dog Owen, reading books from the great theologian Henri Nouwen, enjoying the company of good friends and family, and spending time at her 90-year-old grandmother's house on Sewanee Mountain!

Celtic Evangelism: Fearless Hospitality.
Dale Caldwell

"We have left undone those things which we ought to have done," Anglicans have confessed for centuries, so I should not be surprised by one of the most shameful events of my career as "an evangelist." For years, I hosted a weekly "soup night," to which anyone might come. It was not an overtly Christian event, and many people felt comfortable to come and hang out as they ate soup and bread and drank coffee—usually about a pound of Ethiopian mokka harrar each night.

But one night, I turned a man away. Had he just shown up, I would have said "welcome," but he was brought by a friend who warned me he had been turned away from the shelter for offending women. I called the shelter, who told me more than they should have, and consulted a young woman who had already arrived with her young son, and this one time I said no.

I spread the bad news: One cannot repent; the kingdom of heaven was not at hand. Neither was a bowl of corn chowder on a cold night.

Nor did I hear any news of the kingdom that the man, perhaps an angel unawares, might have had for me. I was ruled by fear rather than love. No man can serve two masters.

Celtic evangelism is not about some spiffy new "worship style." Real Celtic liturgies are almost identical to those used throughout Europe. Celtic evangelism is about opening our lives and our homes to whoever comes, with no fear of the consequences. After all, we have already died in our baptism. But for visiting our homes to be effective in sharing the good news that one can repent, that the kingdom of heaven is at hand, our lives must also be remarkable. But that's probably a story for another time.

Dale has "worn many hats" and is currently living a solitary life and working to recover Celtic Orthodoxy in Fayetteville, Arkansas. More of his work and thoughts may be found at cybermonkblog.wordpress.com.

The Question is Not, "How Can We Grow?"
Nancy Ricketts

As I sat through yet another meeting focused on the decline of membership in the church, I began to wonder if we were merely addressing a symptom and ignoring the life-threatening disease. The fact that more people are walking out the back door than are coming in the front door of both denominational and non-denominational churches in America indicates a serious problem, which won't be solved by flexible worship schedules, expanded visionary statements, or an additional focus group.

The Christian message is a distinct alternative to the culture in which we live. Christ's church is meant to be a community devoted to something greater than us, something exceptional, something that gives life meaning. Christ's church is to be Christ's love incarnate, serving as a representative of God in a world that doesn't know God. Being a Christian involves personal commitment, sacrifice, and accountability. Indeed, it's a lot to ask of someone to live a Christian life and we could understand, perhaps even accept, our declining numbers if prospective members admitted they, like the rich young ruler, simply weren't prepared to make the commitment the Christian faith demands. But in truth, many of those who are walking out our back doors are leaving, not because the commitment they were asked to make was too great, but because it was too small.

Christianity is a relational faith, which relies upon community, emphasizes the common good, pursues peace, and insists upon serving those in need, believing Christ is in each of us. In contrast, American culture worships individualism, heaps praise on those who prosper at the expense of the common good, rationalizes the benefits of war, and regards those in need as societal nuisances. The question is not, "how can we grow?" The question is, "how can we maintain the integrity of the Christian message, while surrounded on every side by a 'me-first' culture?"

The heart of the Christian message can be simply expressed as loving God with our heart, mind, and soul and loving our neighbor as ourselves. Wherever we may be throughout the day, as Christians, all of our actions should reflect these two commandments. This isn't an "either/or" edict; we can't love God and ignore our neighbor, or love our neighbor and ignore God. In fact, these two commandments are reflective of one another. The more we love God, the greater our desire to do what pleases God, which is to serve those in need. The more we serve those in need, the greater our awareness of God's love and our amazement of God's grace. In too many churches, serving those in need is nothing more than another church committee attended to by a small number of members, rather than the very purpose of the church, with a commitment expected from each member of the church to serve others. Such an approach is a "half-church" and no different than if we relegated loving God to a small church committee, while the rest of the membership worked to serve their neighbors.

For generations, the American church has allowed American culture to dilute the Christian message in our desire to be part of the American mainstream. Despite the disparity between the Christian message and the secular message, which encircles the church, and because of a belief the church is destined for a leadership role in America, church authorities have intentionally or unintentionally worked to appease a culture, which is the antithesis of the Christian message. We have become passive, if not active, supporters of American culture, ignoring our God-given role as its prophetic critics. As my grandmother would say, we've been trying to "have our cake and eat it, too," which is reflected by our declining numbers.

For the church to reassume its role as a covenant community, unapologetically working for the common good, loving God, and serving the needs of all of its neighbors, it must focus on commitment to the Christian message, not growth. For the church to truly be Christ's love incarnate, each member of the church must be committed, willing to make personal sacrifices, and hold each other accountable to the difficult task of creating God's Kingdom. I look forward to the day when a visitor to our church admits they aren't sure they're able to make the same commitment and sacrifices they've witnessed of those around them. That's when we will know we are fulfilling our evangelical mission.

Nancy is a Deacon in the Diocese of Texas and she currently serves at St. Michael's Episcopal Church in Austin.

Where are the Oars? *Greg Rickel*

The very notion of a "Boat without Oars" is the picture of a people adrift, letting the currents and winds take us wherever they will. It is a scary way to live, and exciting. But in every age, and in most individual lives, the time comes when oars are needed. We need direction, some focus. So the question might be, "where are the oars?" What are the oars in your life?

So, why the church? What does the church have to offer to people in our communities?

The question is the answer: community. That is what the church has, or should have, to offer to our communities. We live in a time when it is easier to communicate with someone unknown in Germany than it is to walk next door and meet your neighbor. While we have lived through a time when that was almost a welcome thing, I believe it is beginning to wear on our society, and many, especially the young, yearn for a more face-to-face relationship.

When I reflected on this idea of "boats without oars," I kept coming back around to Jesus as my oars, the addition to my travels that gives me direction. Of course, Jesus is my boat, too, keeping me at the surface and safe. Perhaps the oars are the practices I take on in my life so that I have direction, prayer, reflection, meditation, study, mission, surrender. For me, this journey is about traveling without the oars to know what that is like, then, eventually discovering what our oars are. I think the church can, and should, be helping the boats on the water, and those in them, to build their oars.

Greg Rickel is the Bishop of the Diocese of Olympia. You can read his writing at www.bishoprickel.com and www.tens.org.

Come Die With Us. *Josh Hosler*

I'm a student at Virginia Theological Seminary, and I've just finished the required class in church history. Our textbook was the fabulous *Christianity: The First Three Thousand Years* by Diarmaid McCulloch. But while I found the book both all-encompassing and entertaining, I think it might as well bear a snarky subtitle: Christians Behaving Badly. You can tell me all you like that when people burned each other at the stake for heresy, they really meant well and were trying to protect the innocent from hell. But I think such actions prove these people never really understood the Gospel. They didn't trust that God is all-powerful and all-loving. I'm not claiming I would do any better in their shoes, but I do believe God calls us to trust divine power and divine love more than we trust our own. And when we do that, let's be honest: it feels a little like death.

My former rector used to say, "Our mission statement at St. Thomas is 'practicing the hospitality of God.' This is a fine mission statement, but I think a better one would be 'Come die with us.' It wouldn't exactly pack the pews, but it would be the Gospel."

The challenge for Americans and other first-world dwellers in the 21st Century will be that of enoughness. How much money do we really need before we can start giving away what we have? How much power must we shore up, even with good intentions, before we open our hands and allow someone else to share power? How much knowledge are we entitled to be certain of before the time comes to act on what little knowledge we possess? Christians of every stripe talk about "dying daily to self," but how many of us are devoted to daily practices that approach anything remotely resembling death?

This is definitely a challenge for me personally, as I work diligently to make sure my family can pay the bills and try not to go into debt (at all, if possible) while in seminary. I want enough power and control to assure this eventuality. Yet the position in which I find myself is a very privileged one. So far, seminary is something of an island: giving something of myself away to anyone outside the seminary community is optional. This will not be the case once I am ordained, so I'm trying to prepare for this eventuality by watching for opportunities to give money, to give time, to give a listening ear.

What will Christianity become in the remainder of this century? Maybe we can work to make it a place where people can die: where they can surrender their money to someone who needs it more, surrender their power in order to raise others up, and surrender their need to be right. Will this be popular? Of course not. But does it need to be? I expect that many congregations of many denominations will die in the decades to come. How can we help them die gracefully? Will we allow ourselves to be surprised at which of them rise from the dead, and which of them don't?

What if Christianity were to shrink in numbers but grow in influence? *What if Christianity were to die altogether?* Do we believe that would be an unacceptable situation? If so, does that mean we doubt the power of resurrection?

Josh now serves as Assistant Priest (Curate) at St. Paul's Episcopal Church in Bellingham, Washington, where he lives with his wife and daughter, and blogs at http://episcopop.blogspot.com/.

The Woman at the Well. *Janet Davis*

Through the lens of the story of the woman at the well (John 4), I see evangelism as a natural response to a transforming encounter with the Divine. Jesus interrupted this woman's life as he asked her for help. She was further drawn into relationship through his understanding of her deeper thirst, his invitation to authenticity, and his persistence. Real, transforming relationship resulted: "I, the one speaking to you—I am he."

In the wake of that connection, everything was different. The woman who was once so concerned about fetching water, set down her jar. The woman likely avoiding the people by going to the well in the heat of the day, went looking for them. She wanted to celebrate that this man knew everything about her. With her community, she began to ask, "Could this be the Messiah?" (Maybe evangelism is also not all about answers…)

In our largely evangelism-averse tradition, this woman's story raises a new and intriguing question for me: What if our resistance to evangelism is more about a deficit of personal and transforming encounters with the Divine than a lack of courage or fear of vulnerability?

Janet Davis refers to herself as "one who gathers stories." She works as a writer and spiritual director in Austin, Texas. Read more at www.janetdavisonline.com.

Eight Myths about Evangelism. *Carol Morehead*

Evangelism is something that is firmly rooted in the New Testament. Yet the word itself is often laden with mixed—or even negative—reactions and connotations. Still, a central tenet of the Christian faith is the call to share the Good News—or evangelize. What to do?

Perhaps one starting place is to demythologize the concept and try to reclaim it. So here are some common myths about evangelism.

1) I will offend people if I share my faith with them. At times, evangelism has been perceived only as an in-your-face, Are-you-saved? confrontation. But in studies of new Christians, one of the most common reasons given for going to a church is being invited by a friend. Most people, if they have known me very long, will know that I love red, I hate to clean house, and I'm a follower of Jesus Christ. If we begin to really let people know who we are, it's pretty likely that will include letting them know we follow Christ as a central part of our daily life.

2) I don't want to go knock on strangers' doors. Well, join the crowd! Not many of us like to approach strangers that way. The models we find in scripture most often show people sharing their faith with people they know, as part of an ongoing conversation and relationship.

3)I don't know what to say to share my faith. In fact, most of us feel this way. That's partly because faith is sometimes hard to articulate. But *practice makes perfect*. When we begin to share our faith stories with one another *within* the community of faith, it becomes easier to share with our friends and families who are not believers. It can be as simple as saying you'll pray for someone during a time of stress or trouble, or of being a friendly presence. Little steps are the starting point.

4) My faith is personal—I don't think I need to share it. Faith *is* personal but not private. Over and over, God calls people out of their comfort zones to work in the world. As Christians, we are God's hands and feet, and God often works in and through us to reach others. And, here too, when we become comfortable with sharing among ourselves, we then begin to open ourselves in surprising new ways.

5) People will think I'm judging them if I talk to them about God. Evangelism isn't about telling someone what's right. It is about sharing what you have experienced in your own life—and what difference it has made. Sharing our faith is grounded in relationship. I have a friend who used to always react with an excuse or like she felt guilty if I spoke about church activities or about prayer. She would say "Well I know I should go back to church" or "God probably would strike me down if I ever prayed again." Because we are friends, we have had some great discussions about why she might feel that way. And I've been able to say that I don't experience God that way, and I believe she would be welcomed with open arms should she ever choose to go to a church. She knows now, feels safe enough with me, to understand that I don't judge her. Rather, I care for her and love her, and I want only good in her life, and for me that includes God.

6) I'm not sure if I believe in hell or that people go to hell; so why do I need to tell others about God? Certainly, a big motivator for many Christians to evangelize is the hope of heaven or fear of hell. Yet there are many of us who believe that being a Christian makes a clear difference in our day-to-day lives, here and now. Being a Christian means *living now* in the way God calls us to be, to act and react in all things as a part of God's kingdom. And if heaven or hell comes up, it's ok to have different understandings of what that might be.

7) I'm not good with words. Can't I just give to my church and let someone else evangelize? While we, as Christians, are called to share our material blessings, we are also called to share our faith. This happens in big and small ways, through our actions and our words. It isn't enough to just support the church financially; we are called to give ourselves to God every day, in all we do. How does that translate into evangelism? It means that we treat people we meet differently, that we have hope in the face of hopelessness, that we invest ourselves in the lives of those around us, that we work for a better world, that we speak about the hope we have.

8) That's the job of the priest or pastor. This is a common feeling. Yet our baptismal vows *couldn't* be clearer: we are *all* called to be evangelists, to share our faith in word and deed, day by day, hour by hour. The priest or pastor is often the face up front. But most people don't come to a church for the pastor; they come because a friend, a neighbor, a colleague invited them.

The New Testament, in the words of St. Peter, encourages us to be ready to speak about our faith: "Always be prepared to give an answer to everyone who asks you to give the reason for the hope that you have. But do this with gentleness and respect." (I Peter 3:15) When Jesus Christ is our Lord, we *do* have hope. Now *that's* something to talk about!

Carol is the associate rector at St. Mark's Episcopal Church in San Antonio, Texas. She shares her life with her husband, three sons, two dogs, and two cats. Their house has a lot of pizza, jazz, laughter, and Led Zeppelin, plus volumes and volumes of books, mostly about God and kung fu.

Questions

What five words would you choose to describe the future of the church?

How does the church tell the world that there really is Resurrection?

How do we evangelize in what some have called "our culture of fear?"

What "Good News" do you proclaim?

How does your church care for the spiritual needs of children?

What tools equip a church to evangelize well?

MAY 2012: THE JOURNEY BEGINS

Our ship has sailed. Early on Saturday morning, heavily laden with clothes for many seasons and geographies, multiple sets of crayons and colored pencils, many items ultimately rejected due to the inability of the trunk to close, we embarked to the east. The parting was bittersweet. We closed the door on our freshly cleaned house and walked away from a whole host of comforts for both adults and children. For the next three months, gone is the comfort of cooking with our favorite set of cast-iron skillets, sleeping between familiar sheets, playing with favorite dolls and toys. Gone is the familiarity of our neighborhood, our local communities of worship. There have been many goodbyes this week. However, on the other side of this trepidation is the thrill of adventure, the excitement of what we may discover on this journey, all of the new people and "hellos."

We walked out of our house and locked the door. Then we stood in our driveway, said a prayer, and paraded around our Toyota Camry with an icon we carry along with us on extended vacations, one of Jesus and the travelers on the Emmaus Road. We prayed for our car, ourselves, and all of the people we were journeying to meet. We hung a pendant from our rear-view mirror, given to us just the day before from fresh Seminary graduates, moving back to New Zealand. The pendant is the Maori symbol for eternal emerging paths, of unity. This symbol represents our most fervent prayer for our family on this journey, and is a visual reminder of friends new and old.

—**Kristin**

"Triskelions" are ancient, pre-Celtic symbols that Christian Celts later incorporated as a symbol of the Trinity or eternity. Image from public domain.

Embrace the World. *Michael*

A few weeks ago, I shared a lunch table with Jonny Baker from the Church Mission Society in England. He was visiting Austin for South by Southwest and he and author Becky Garrison stopped by the seminary to host a roundtable discussion about mission. The group of us had a wonderful discussion about how to "do church" in ways that appeal to people who wouldn't ordinarily come. In the course of this conversation, we talked extensively about Fresh Expressions: a part of the Church of England's missional strategy. Fresh Expressions was born out of the observation that the church was sending missionaries to places like Africa and doing really well; in fact, the African churches were doing better than the ones in England, so the Church Mission Society decided to concentrate its efforts locally. They began to pay attention to the generational disconnect which had emptied their churches and realized that in reaching out to a whole new population, they were going to have to think quite differently.

The resources they settled on are quite interesting: they studied stories from the 19th-Century missionaries to natives in America and Africa. In retelling the stories of evangelizing the Masai people of Africa, or the Lakota Sioux of the American plains, these leaders found illumination and inspiration for how to express the gospel message in ways that connected with the culture of English youth. Jonny said that the goal in all such mission work was "an indigenous expression of Christianity with indigenous leadership," and if done well enough could actually facilitate "a re-theologizing from a new context." Such a boldly contextual picture of what evangelism can be is inspiring…and easily lost in a place like the church, where we feel so tied to each jot and tittle of our understanding of faith that each reimagining can feel like a threat to the very core of our belief.

At its base, Christianity has always been about discerning a truly localized expression of faith: that is why we have preserved so much of Roman thought and culture in our worship, theology, and calendar. Rome was the locality, which for better or worse: "took," and continues to dominate so much of Western society. Evangelism, then, is first about finding the good that is already there—in Roman culture then; and in online communities, hipster culture, urban homesteading, hip-hop, etc. now—and then reconnecting that good to Christ through worship and service within that particular community. For the church to go into new mission fields with the primary goal of exposing sin or contradicting deeply held patterns and beliefs is counterproductive; even harmful. Jonny told us instead to find ways to be more at home in the culture than in church: don't be afraid of what's out there—embrace the world.

Evangelism as Spiritual Practice. *Michael*

The clichéd sweaty televangelist and his "ministry" of heavy-handed emotional extortion is more than just a caricature of a fading era; it is the first thing people think about when they hear the word "evangelism." This is the baggage that comes along with the Great Commission: our faith gets lumped together with hucksterism and sales pitches of the lowest order. To the degree that the church continues to accept this vernacular injustice, we are robbed of a practice that creates and sustains the identity of our communal faith. Evangelism is more than an exercise in metaphysical marketing; it is the ancient spiritual practice of meaning-making: of telling our world and ourselves into being.

While faith is an inexpressible participation in divine reality, religion lives and dies on vocabulary. The vast demographic shift to "spiritual, but not religious" is a nod to the evacuation of meaning in Christian terminology. This, of course, is the danger of attempting to name the unnamable. The words of faith are volatile by nature, and they can be bent from the plowshares of hospitality and mutual conversation to the swords of domination and exclusion with only a little effort. In our generation, this process has severed evangelism from its connection with Good News and confined it to a popular conception of something which seems neither "good" nor "new," sending mainline Christians scrambling to hide their lamps under baskets (Luke 11:33).

The Christian faith, however, is intended to be out in the open, and words play a key role in the display. Evangelism, then, indicates a practice of mindfulness with words. Just as I must learn a few chords before I am ready to play a guitar, I must learn a few words before I can explore my spirituality. Worship provides a rich source of such words in the form of scripture, prayer, reflection, and action, and through repeated encounters, I begin to take on the vocabulary of religion. The terms and stories I find most troubling often reveal the deepest parts of myself, and—as I hear others wrestling with the same words—I discover the richness of this holy language. Over time, the words of religion shape us to view all of life with the conviction that God is active among us.

This lens prepares us for a more interactive practice of evangelism. Taking comfort in the knowledge that our task is to discover (rather than define) what God is doing, God's work becomes apparent in the lives of our neighbors and friends. The odd words and strange stories of religion become stepping-stones to spiritual conversations of mutual hospitality: an exchange characterized more by listening than telling, by sharing the joy and pain of real life experiences instead of spiritualizing or abstracting the meaning of others' lives. Evangelism becomes a discipline of personal conversion: of seeing yourself through the eyes of your community, of seeing God through the eyes of your neighbor.

Our faith defies confinement to a simple campaign or a list of propositions. Attempts to restrict it—usually wearing the guise of evangelism (i.e. "Four Steps to Salvation")—depict a brittle, anemic belief. Instead of sound bites or heavy-handed emotional appeals, evangelism is a practice: a habit of deeply examining our own spirituality through engaging the spirituality of others. Through mutual exploration, we realize more fully our identity as people on a journey with God, and we can offer to others our sincere invitation to join us. Evangelism is a gift to the world whereby we join others as they fathom their place in creation, and locate our own in their reflection.

Photo credit: Kristin Carroccino. Keep the Conversation Going.
Decatur, Alabama. April 2011.

A Sense of Place: Decatur, Alabama, and St. John's Episcopal Church. *Kristin*

Decatur is a community of 55,000 people located about halfway between Nashville, Tennessee, and Birmingham, Alabama. I grew up in this town, and it was a good place to be a child. Parks and churches are plentiful; the schools are good, and the community, for the most part, is close-knit. The city's most recent self-proclaimed slogan is "A Grand City on a Charming Scale," and I think this phrase perfectly captures how most Decatur residents feel about their hometown. Past monikers have included "The River City" and "Home of Meow Mix"—both are still true.

On these early summer mornings, we wake to the sounds of raucous bird symphonies, lawn mowers, and distant train whistles. A faint scent of soybeans wafts through the air, drifting from the riverside factories that process the local crop and convert it into pet foods and other products. Residents of Decatur take pride in well-maintained tidy, green lawns; gardens full of azaleas, magnolias, and gardenias perfume the air. Many people exercise here on biking and hiking trails. On most mornings and evenings, a faithful parade of walkers and bikers stream by the house where I spent my entire childhood, and where my parents still reside.

People feel proud to be "from" Decatur. There is a history of citizens working together to further civic progress or joining to preserve moral traditions. Decatur was mostly demolished during the Civil War and then rebuilt in the 1880s. In the early Twentieth Century, citizens of "Old" and "New" Decatur overcame deep historic animosity to marshal resources and build a bridge to replace the ferry service spanning the Tennessee River. Later, Decatur was the largest city for many years that was "dry," not permitting the sale of alcohol within city limits until the 1980s. I remember when I was very young, most businesses were closed on Sundays, another mark of community pride.

Constancy, consistency, loyalty, and beautification are words that come to mind as I look back over my experience of growing up in Decatur, and what I observe upon return. In over thirty years, the cultural mix has changed little, though more modern industries and proximity to the Redstone Arsenal and NASA-related space and defense industries in nearby Huntsville have created cultural diversity that is unique to this part of Alabama.

Keeping up appearances and traditions and being sociable are integral to being a thriving member of this community. Behind the beautiful lawns, cars, and clothing is a resolute grit. People in Decatur have a keen sense of what they know to be "right," which can sometimes create conflict, but more often than not, this determination raises in defense of the wronged or vulnerable, so that churches of most denominations here are very loving and generous within their own membership, as well as toward the broader community. Church and "being Christian," no matter to which denomination one belongs, is very much socially dominant. City streets are almost empty during Sunday worship hours, and restaurants have long wait times following the conclusion of 11 a.m. church services.

St. John's Episcopal Church, founded in 1890, stands proudly at an elegant angle to downtown Decatur, not far from the city center, rail yard, and Farmer's Market, where the current crop of tomatoes, peaches, strawberries, and broccoli are sold on every day but Sunday. I grew up as a Southern Baptist and visited St.

John's only once during my youth, with a high school boyfriend. I distinctly remember the beautiful silver chalice used to serve the Communion wine and the white-robed choir processing in and out and surrounding all of us with heavenly voices. It was a feast for my senses that was tucked away to be remembered over twenty years later when I again knelt at the altar rail this morning as part of our visit to study St. John's for *Boats without Oars*.

In my exploration of how a city's culture and history may shape a church's character, I find that the parishioners at St. John's represent the

photo: Kristin Carroccino. St. John's May 2012

essence of Decatur. They are warm and graceful, generous in their giving, and very proud to be Episcopalians. Many are civic and business leaders known in Decatur to be members of St. John's, a membership that carries a sense of honor. St. John's seems to be increasingly inviting. New, well-marked signs point the way to the Episcopal Outreach Center that houses a community health clinic. Community garden spaces and a small playground crowned by a miniature steeple fill the green space around the church campus.

On this Sunday, we begin the working part of our travels. It is "youth Sunday," an occasion, usually near the end of a school year, which honors people graduating from high school or college. A well-spoken, about-to-graduate high school senior delivers the homily, offering words full of hope and challenge to her peers for the years ahead. Michael will be preaching many Sundays this summer, sharing with listeners the vision for our project and the stories we are collecting. Today, however, Fr. Evan Garner introduces us and asks us to briefly remark about the reason for our visit. Families with young children visiting Episcopal churches rarely go unnoticed; we are no exception.

Mirella clings to my legs as the four of us amble to the lectern. When Michael introduces us, Caedmon grabs the microphone and babbles something mostly incomprehensible, which garners chuckles from everyone but us. This awkward introduction is how we begin our first parish visit; we are humbled by our nervousness about announcing our summer project, and by the unexpected fervor of our young son to broadcast his voice to the masses.

And we're off! The *Boats without Oars* interviews begin tomorrow; we are eager to begin collecting stories and testing our theory that growth and life are abundant in Episcopal churches. Decatur and St. John's are a fine place to begin.

"We're the Church that Feeds People." St. John's Episcopal Church, Decatur, Alabama. *Michael*

"St. John's has done more outreach wise than—in my bumping around—I've seen in a church this size."

This came from a man who has lived all over the world and worshiped in many places, and his passion for finding ways to "love your neighbor as yourself" shined throughout my interview with him. In a nutshell, this church has a strong and close-knit group who are very engaged in the needs of the underserved in Decatur, though many people outside of St. John's are unaware of this generosity. Parishioners work and serve faithfully their city both vocationally and voluntarily; I met several nurses, teachers, and social workers in my interviews. They give their personal and communal funds to an astounding variety of community programs that provide for the needs of many in their neighborhood. The people of St. John's love Decatur, and they are proud to be Episcopalians and proud of their church.

"We feed, we worship, and we eat together."

Among the many topics covered in my interviews, food seemed to top the list at this church! "Come to my church! We'll feed you fried chicken!" Eating is a common parish activity for St. John's, and at any major event they are likely to be found gathered around the table. They meet consistently on Wednesday nights to cook (they do this in a rotation of teams) and eat meals together, and almost everybody shows up. They give food out in a variety of ways: they pack backpacks of food for local school kids to take home over the weekend, they grow food in a community garden ("it's our bridge to the community"), their kids bake cookies for local emergency workers, and they deliver meals to one another in times of need. Many of the people I interviewed were quick to connect this facet of their community to their worship, and several brought up the idea of being spiritually "fed" as being part of their vision of what church should be.

"We should buy that building—who's in with me?"

One day at a parish officers meeting, a man stood at the window looking out at the dilapidated hospital building next door, and issued a challenge. The idea had been brewing for a while, and it took years to come to fruition, but the Episcopal

Outreach Center is now perhaps the most visible symbol of St. John's commitment to providing for their neighbors. In its two floors are housed—"we don't charge any rent!"—the Free Clinic from the local hospital and Parents and Children Together, a family resource center. It took a lot of work, a lot more money than they ever expected, and the dedication of parish leaders, accountants, and lawyers to pull it off, but they did it, and they were happy to give their efforts in service to the needs of Decatur. Some of the parishioners volunteer at the center on a regular basis, but others are already looking for the next big defining project for St. John's.

"How important it is for all of us to sit together, kneel together, pray together."

Christian formation is very strong at St. John's—people here find themselves involved in a variety of Bible studies, guilds, EFM, and education classes; and they love spending the time together and the things they learn. Many of those I interviewed were hesitant to talk about evangelism, but as a group, they abound in ability to talk about their faith and apply it to their daily lives. One woman told me that other local congregations had tried to tell her preteen children they could leave their parents' church and worship on their own—but she would not be put off so easily: worship is a family affair and she is committed to their continuance together in their faith. Parishioners at St. John's take the faith they learn together "to work, to family, to parenting—and live it," and they are well able to connect it to events in the world around them.

"I love this church."

All the stories I heard centered on how familiar this church is. People know each other's name, "the priest knows your name," and they just generally enjoy one another's company. When asked what exemplifies the community of St. John's, one woman said, "all of us out back gathered around watching the kids play." They learn together, they eat together, they worship together, and they take care of each other. St. John's has much innate strength as a parish to devote toward whatever they put their minds to next. They face the same challenges as much of the church—their statistics are not much different from national averages—but they are not afraid to look at their difficulties and work together to overcome them. All over a big plate of fried chicken.

Outreach in our Parish. *Evan Garner*

Father Evan Garner is the rector at St. John's Episcopal in Decatur, Alabama. He began his tenure at St. John's in the Fall of 2011 after spending almost six years as an associate rector at St. John's in Montgomery, Alabama. We began our summer of parish studies with St. John's and asked Fr. Evan to respond to the following question:

"How do the outreach programs in your parish affect the spirituality of individual parishioners?"

I've told the story many times, but it's worth at least one more telling. On my first Wednesday night at St. John's, I got a sense of how important outreach is to our parish. During the announcements, I heard calls for volunteers to serve lunch at a soup kitchen and dinner at a transitional housing facility, for donations of shoes for one organization and toys for another, and for gifts of time and support for yet another ongoing outreach ministry of the parish. Five different requests for help all on the same night!

That dizzying display of commitment to outreach told me a lot about our church. First, it showed me that we care about the community and want to be involved in ministries that make a difference in the lives of those in need. Second, it showed me that lots of different individuals support lots of different projects. Finally, it revealed that we need to find a unifying thread that pulls all of our disparate work together.

At St. John's, outreach programs are a vital part of individuals' spirituality. I've seen people's faith come alive when they connect with a local agency and work alongside others to help God's kingdom grow. Unfortunately, those efforts are often too individualized. Although members of St. John's go out in twos and threes to make a difference in the world, that work isn't always connected back to the work of our parish as a whole. Making that transition from a collection of parts to a well-coordinated whole might be as easy as naming that as a priority for our parish or enabling communication between the separate groups. Foundationally, the commitment of individuals to outreach is the liveliest expression of faith or spirituality I've seen so far at St. John's, but I'm looking forward to watching deeper connections within our community grow.

Interview: Fr. Bill King. Trinity Episcopal Church, Clanton, Alabama. *Kristin*

Trinity Episcopal Church in Clanton, Alabama, sits a few blocks off Main Street and just a few steps away from where Michael's parents used to live. Trinity's reputation and influence in the small town of Clanton has been growing dramatically over the last few years. A cousin of Michael's lives six months of the year in Clanton, and told us recently that Trinity has become known as the "beans and rice church." We decided we would like to visit the parish and interview the current rector, Father Bill King, to learn more.

Bill King has served various capacities in the Diocese of Alabama and Central Gulf Coast Diocese. He started his career as a Roman Catholic priest and later became an Episcopalian minister. Bill seems to have a deep passion for the health of the Diocese as a whole, and while working in the bishop's office, he started looking at areas in Alabama that "should" have an Episcopal presence. Clanton was one of those communities. This large town of around 5,000 residents is situated about halfway between the much larger cities of Birmingham and Montgomery. Trinity Episcopal Church had shut its doors decades before, and the building was serving as a daycare when Bill came to visit it in the early 1990s. Things were about to change.

After working with leadership from St. Marks's in nearby Prattville, Bill King and a few volunteers rented a couple of rooms at the Clanton Holiday Inn, got a stack of phone books, and started cold-calling people in the Clanton area to tell them about Episcopalianism and about what was about to begin at Trinity Episcopal. A few dedicated members helped things begin to grow slowly. Father Bill, still working for the Diocese, watched from afar, and in 2003 made the transition to being the new rector at Trinity. In that year, there was still no budget, only ten members, and Bill only drove down from Birmingham on Sundays for services, inviting a few of his Birmingham friends and a musician to join him for the weekly commute to worship in Clanton. The extra people in the pews from Birmingham added more variety and richness to the worship experience. People in Clanton began to notice.

Bill has been very creative and pragmatic in helping Trinity to thrive, even in the way he appoints the inside of the building. He has paid attention and utilized Diocesan contacts to purchase at reduced cost, or request by donation, sets of dishes when parishes have closed. He has acquired beautiful icons and other sacred art for this tiny space in the same way. Maintaining a beautiful worship space is integral to Bill's style of worship and is probably one of the first changes he initiated in 2003. He began to infuse the congregation with energy by placing importance and pride in maintaining the building, so much so that by 2005, a man who was deaf paid $1,600 for a used bell for the church that he would never himself be able to hear. In 2006, a new-used set of pews was installed, and a new altar was built using donated funds. In 2007, a new bathroom, kitchen, and central heating and air conditioning were furnished. Bill has donors on the ready around the state of Alabama to provide new prayer books and hymnals as needed. In 2009, Trinity changed its status from "worshiping community" to "parish," and by fall of 2011, membership had blossomed to around 80 people. In addition to Sundays, Fr. Bill now drives down every Wednesday to participate in various community offerings, such as a monthly men's prayer breakfast, monthly healing service, or monthly potluck lunch. There are a lot of parties and shared meals around Trinity these days. Parishioners have their own personal key to unlock the church's nave.

Photo, Kristin Carroccino. Trinity Episcopal Church, Clanton, Alabama. May 2012.

What has been driving this growth? The revitalization seems to be a healthy combination of Bill's energetic leadership and conviction, and the hard work and hospitality of the laity. During his diocesan work, Bill developed a list of "Ten Things to Do Well in Growing and Instilling Healthy Life into a Small Church" that sums up his approach to the difference in leading small communities compared to larger parishes.

In addition to applying a different leadership approach to a small congregation, Bill also believes growth is happening at Trinity, Clanton, for several reasons: consistently promoting the uniqueness of the Episcopal tradition (a sacramental liturgy, introduction of iconography), offering stability by employing the same priest for a number of years, working to empower lay people and raising up lay leaders, seeking to avoid controversy, focusing on meeting as a worshiping community, living with the mindset of abundance and not scarcity, and emphasizing that "all people are welcome." He insists on "good liturgy" and involving all attendees in worship. On Sundays, each child who attends is invited to wear a robe and carry something in the procession. Everyone of every age and gender around here is appreciated as a leader. To emphasize Bill's strong belief in the role of women in leadership, Trinity's new deacon always wears her collar. Bill firmly believes that "small churches shouldn't get the hand-me-downs" and turns away donations that aren't beautiful and appropriate to Trinity's needs. One of Bill's wisest insights is to appreciate where growth is possible and let things die away at the appropriate time. He says that "dying churches are in dying communities," and that, "the flowering of the church is but for a season," pointing to the fact that the famous Corinthians to which Paul wrote in the First Century had ceased to exist as a church by the Second Century.

Most notably, Bill says that Trinity really "made it" a few years back when they started looking outward and began doing things for others in the community and not just themselves. Six years ago, the church started a beans-and-rice ministry, offering on a monthly basis dried beans and rice for local families in need. This ministry has now expanded to offering provisions to many families in the area. Bill also chooses as much as possible to be active in the community life of Clanton and supports local businesses For example, he chooses to get his hair cut in Clanton instead of in Birmingham (about an hour north) where he still resides. In fact, the first time Bill walked into the hair salon, his new stylist exclaimed, "oh, you're the beans-and-rice church pastor!"

Trinity Church is an inspiration. There is growth happening inside the doors and spilling out onto the streets, not just with beans and rice, but even in the recently added "Biblical herb garden" on the grounds that invites people strolling by to stop and ponder. An outdoor Stations of the Cross is offered multiple times during the year. Trinity also collaborates with other worshiping congregations in Clanton. During Holy Week, the local Catholic community and Trinity process together across several city blocks. Trinity Episcopal is a success story, and we feel invigorated and thankful to have spent time listening to Bill's stories. We gained many new insights into how one leader and a handful of people acted in faith, practiced evangelism, and helped create a thriving community.

Image from the Diocese of Alabama website: www.dioala.ort/dave/hunger.html.

Ten Things to do Well in Growing and Instilling Healthy Life Into a Small Church. *William M. King,* **2011©**

PREFACE

Over half of all Episcopal Church parishes have an average Sunday attendance of less than 75 persons. Average Sunday attendance below 75 persons is a very important piece of information in defining small church. Many small parishes, missions or worshipping communities are in rural areas where there is very little growth potential, but other small congregations are either in older inner city/urban settings beginning to see some redevelopment or in rural growth areas on the fringe of metropolitan areas where suburban or exurban growth is beginning to have positive impact. To better support the small church, it is important for dioceses within the Episcopal Church to develop an active strategy for small church development for three reasons: First, it is evangelism at its best because it plants or retains the Episcopal Church tradition for the future in a very inexpensive way. Second, if the Episcopal Church is not present in towns between 5,000 and 10,000 in population, there will be a significant number of Episcopalians who will be forced by neglect and absence of our church to join other Christian traditions or become part of the un-churched. Third, small church experience can be extremely rich and rewarding for the entire church because pastoral care is personal, community visibility of the church so clearly defined and leadership is often shared by a wide base within the parish.

The following material outlines ten things to do well to help small rural or urban churches grow or at least maintain a healthy position. All of what I write in this article comes from seven years of direct ministry at Trinity Church, Clanton in the Diocese of Alabama and working to establish other small town churches in the Diocese of Alabama between 1998 and 2007 when I served as Deputy to the Bishop for Congregational Development and Clergy Deployment. In 2004, Trinity Episcopal Church, Clanton had 12 active members and an average attendance of less than 10. In 2011, the congregation had 72 active members AND averaging 42 persons in attendance every Sunday. In great part, the growth of this congregation has come about by the realization that steady development takes place as a result of hard, energized, patient and faithful work on the part of all of its members. I have often referred to Trinity Church as "the little church that can."

1. DEVELOP A HEALTHY WELCOMING MINISTRY.

Several years ago, a New York Times article titled "An Unlikely Mega church Lesson" (11/3/07) spoke about Jewish leaders seeking out the secrets of evangelical success. Much of the article had to do with how seekers or newcomers were welcomed into a faith community. A small church may have difficulty establishing a specialized welcoming committee, but it can assign its vestry members to regularly rotate as greeters outside/inside the front door of the church. Small churches may get one visitor at a time and the vestry greeter can both welcome and sit with the visitor(s) in designated seating, being sure that the visitor can follow the service and that a visitor's card is filled out and dropped into the alms basin. A written note from the rector in the week following an initial visit is also critical. Another aspect of welcoming is the wearing of name tags for everyone every Sunday or perhaps by designating one Sunday a month as "Name Tag" Sunday. Proper welcoming is essential for church growth.

2. MAINTAIN AN ACTIVE WEB PAGE AND PARISH E-MAIL LIST

Persons under the age of 50 now primarily make use of Google, Facebook, Twitter and other active social media sites to find information, directions, photographs, current sermons or desired resources. It is not difficult for a small church to establish and maintain several active web sites. Active is the key word. If you are not willing to constantly update your web site, no less than once or twice a week, don't have one. Static information is not welcoming information and web site visitors will not come back for a second look. Electronic mailing lists also are extremely helpful ways to actively communicate with members of the parish and visitors with reminders, pastoral information, and spiritual messages on a regular mid-week basis.

3. WORSHIP SPACE MUST BE WELL DESIGNED

People are seeking spiritual experiences today that are prayerful and that reflect more of the historic traditions of the entire church. Worship space must be clean, uncluttered, with good lighting and easily recognized as a place set aside for prayer and worship. When people walk into a church they are not so concerned about size as they are interested in connecting with the holy, the sacred with a sense of awe and mystery. In the Episcopal tradition, altar, baptismal font with water in it, ambo (a single lectern) and bishops chair are the essentials, according to the late Rev. Dr. Marion Hatchett, professor of Liturgy at the Univ. of the South. Cluttered space leads to distraction and poorly maintained space can be one more reason why some people will not come back for a second visit. And poor lighting may keep older members from attending evening worship services such as Christmas Eve or Ash Wednesday.

4. ADVERTISE, ADVERTISE, ADVERTISE

There are lots of available free local advertising and publicity outlets. Local newspapers publish free articles and photographs about events, celebrations and ministries and often invite pastors to write an occasional inspirational article. Visit the local newspaper publisher to find out what might be possible. Time on a local radio or cable TV station is often very inexpensive. For several years, Calvary Episcopal Church in Oneonta, Alabama, a 40 member congregation, paid $1 per minute for 15 minutes every Sunday morning on a local radio station where the sermon for that Sunday was delivered together with a prayer for the week. Signage directing people to the church is also important advertising, but it must be kept current and clean. Finding the church is the first step in getting visitors in the front door.

5. HAVE AN OUTREACH MINISTRY FOR WHICH YOUR PARISH IS KNOWN

I strongly believe that small churches should not try to mimic larger churches in programs or ministries, but rather creatively carry out ministries that are manageable and exciting to them and for which they become known in the community. For instance, Grace Episcopal Church (Woodlawn) in Birmingham, a parish of about 130 members, maintains a food pantry for those in need of food. It is open once a week and staffed by parish volunteers. Grants and gifts have been received to renovate space and buy shelving for the pantry. Larger parishes now assist Grace in their ministry. Trinity, Clanton offers free beans and rice to anyone in need on the 1st Saturday morning of each month. 1st Saturdays have now become a parish work day as well at Trinity, often bringing together no less than 10 members of the parish doing various work assignments together. Being known for one significant ministry to the community is more meaningful than attempting to do several outreach projects halfway or just giving money in a "pass through" effort to work carried out by others.

6. REMEMBER THAT CALLING PEOPLE TO PRAYER AND WORSHIP IS ALWAYS NUMBER ONE

The idea of a bell at the church has to do with calling the community to prayer. The church bell is a reminder that first and foremost, the church is a place of prayer, not just for one hour on Sunday, but as often as possible. Morning Prayer, Centering Prayer, Holy Eucharist or Compline are prayer services which might take place on any day of the week and any hour of the day. It is important to remind the entire community that we are a place of prayer for all people and a place that will welcome all people. Keep the lights on and ring the church bell whenever prayers are being offered in the church. The entire community will begin to notice the association between the bell ringing and the call to prayer.

7. EVERYONE HAS A MINISTRY

It is certainly an understatement to say that in a small church everyone counts. But also everyone needs to be involved in at least one ministry so that everyone feels included and valued. It is healthier to have different Eucharistic Ministers, readers and ushers for each week of the month rather than the same few carrying out these roles every Sunday. Vestry members should not be the only parishioners invited to take on roles in worship or outreach or Christian Formation. It takes every member to keep a small church functioning and that is a healthy model to follow.

8. PLAN FOR GROWTH

A plan for growth might be as simple as every parish family being asked to invite one guest to church once a quarter (every three months). Most newcomers enter the doors of the church by invitation of a member of the parish than by any other way. It is not the priest who gets people into the church, it is the laity. Growth requires intentional planning and lots of conversation. It may also require someone from the diocese being invited as a consultant to assist with the conversation. Planning for growth begins with prayer followed by decisions about ministry design and only then should facility planning take place. But when the church nave regularly becomes 75% full on Sunday morning, the parish needs to begin planning either for an additional Sunday service or expand the seating capacity of its church nave. At Trinity, Clanton an additional 10 seats (including one rocking chair for mothers with infants) were added at a cost of $7,000 by enlarging the footprint of worship space by 4 feet and redesigning the sanctuary area around the altar.

9. COORDINATION WITH OTHER SMALL CONGREGATIONS

Small parishes can come together in a variety of ways to create and support ministry, such as a shared Parish Retreat, a regional EFM class, shared evening time family Vacation Bible School, sexual conduct training for parish volunteers, shared Lessons and Carols in Advent, a Taize service or a shared picnic at a lake house. Clergy from adjoining small congregations might meet together for sermon planning and fellowship or pastoral support once a month. Being intentional about sharing and cooperating is what is important, thus remembering that a small parish is also connected with the larger church within a diocese.

10. MUSIC MINISTRY REFLECTING THE SIZE OF THE CONGREGATION

A mistake often made by a small congregation is that of attempting to mimic a music ministry of the large parish. An organ is not essential to good liturgical music. A choir is not essential for good liturgical music. What is important is a commitment to good liturgical music as part of public worship with sufficient space set aside in the church for a musician and cantor (song leader). An excellent key board musician plus a well trained cantor who can lead and encourage the congregation in both the singing of hymns and of psalms contributes much to prayerful worship. This beginning can be augmented on special occasions and feast days by violin or cello or flute or perhaps a four to eight person choir singing a more difficult hymn as an anthem. As the church grows, the music ministry will also grow in a manner most fitting to the size of the congregation.

This document is used with permission from Rev. Bill King of Trinity Episcopal Church in Clanton, Alabama. For permission to reprint, please contact Rev. Bill via the Trinity website at http://trinityepiscopalchurch.dioala.org/.

A Sense of Place: Atlanta and Church of the Holy Comforter. *Kristin*

Historically, Atlanta was once called the "City of the New South," a phrase that described the city's rise from the ashes of Civil War decimation well over a century ago, when local officials began to promote their city's departure from agriculture and the slave system that brought prosperity to Atlanta, to more modern styles of commerce. As we drive through Atlanta this week, we commute via five lanes of highway gridlock beneath tall downtown skyscrapers, including one topped with a peach and another with the sculpture of the Olympic Flame, a permanent memorial to the Games held here in 1996. It is easy to forget Atlanta's agrarian beginnings. Home to the world's largest indoor aquarium, the World of Coke, headquarters of CNN and The Weather Channel, Atlanta is an increasingly global city.

The Chattahoochee River meanders its way through the heart of the city, where locals still throng on the weekends, drawn to its wide shoals. I once hiked to the headwaters of the Chattahoochee to fill my water bottle while backpacking along the Appalachian Trail in north Georgia with a friend. The muddy trickle we found at the end of the steep trail belies the broad, flowing river we walk beside today. Hikers, bikers, paddlers, bird watchers, and anglers mingle along its banks, within view of the downtown glass-and-steel skyline. Those towers of commerce also look down upon the homes of Margaret Mitchell, author of *Gone with the Wind*, and the home of and first church where Martin Luther King, Jr., preached. We sat inside Ebenezer Baptist Church on a hot Saturday afternoon and listened to recorded sermons of its most famous preacher, while a raucous Caribbean street festival erupted in sound and color on the surrounding neighborhood streets. Atlanta is a study in contrasts: old and new, wealthy and impoverished, natural and manufactured.

Within the churches of the Episcopal Diocese of Atlanta, the contrasts continue—from large, wealthy parishes downtown and in the suburbs—to places like the mission Church of the Holy Comforter, the site of our second parish visit for *Boats without Oars*. Near the edge of eastern Atlanta, where we drive through newly gentrifying neighborhoods not far from Candler Park and Emory University, locales where community land trusts and gardens and cohousing communities are increasingly in vogue, Church of the Holy Comforter rests on several green and rambling acres with a large sign proclaiming that "All Are Welcome."

As we pulled into the parking lot for the first time, I was instantly aware that Holy Comforter was a church unlike any I have visited. People of all colors and physical and mental capabilities were milling about in the parking lot and boarding large, white church vans. We parked between the vans in front of a sturdy greenhouse and sprawling vegetable garden. People greeted us as friends, patting us on the back, big smiles, full of spirit. We soon learned that most of these people were just finishing their day at the Friendship Center, a program administered by Holy Comforter that reaches out to people with chronic mental illness, and provides a haven of community for a population largely left behind by mainstream society.

photo: *Kristin Carroccino, Church of the Holy Comforter, Atlanta, Georgia, May 2012.*

In the halls below Holy Comforter's simple but beautiful nave, paintings by Friendship Center participants line the walls. Everything is alive with color here—the people we meet, the gardens, the paintings. A stroll through the corridors and a glance at the bulletin boards reveal announcements about outreach projects, environmental stewardship awards, and sign-up sheets for keeping common spaces tidy. Parts of the Friendship Center program have moved off-site as membership has grown, and about a mile away in a Baptist church basement, attendees can take painting, weaving, pottery, woodworking, knitting, or jewelry-making classes. Participants' art is sold in shows throughout the year to help sustain the Friendship Center program. Yoga, music classes, hand-and foot-care clinics, meals, and noon prayer are other offerings for the Center's attendees, who gather each Tuesday and Thursday.

Holy Comfort seems to follow us around during our visit. Our children are peaceful and playful in a colorful childcare room where they enjoy toys and books while Michael and I meet and share dinner with the vestry during their monthly meeting, and later as we interview Father Mike Tanner and his wife Cozette in the office next door. Mike's office is warm and inviting: beaded board paneling painted in a warm color, Mike and Cozette talking to both of us, rocking quietly in their chairs, listening, and sharing. I don't feel like I am inside a church, but rather sitting in someone's living room. During our interview and in the vestry meeting, I became increasingly aware of the passion and determination Holy Comforter's leadership team has for sustaining its ministry to Friendship Center. Parishioners represent a wide range of socio-economic levels but share their desire to worship with, and provide care for, Friendship Center's community. During our few days at this parish, every person I spoke with was energetic about his or her ministry, whether weeding in the community garden, planning an art sale, or complaining about the task of sorting through the growing mounds of clothing donated to Friendship Center.

Does Atlanta shape the community of Church of the Holy Comforter? I think so. In this city of contrasts, there is always the constant of southern hospitality. We received it from the moment we parked beside the big, white vans on the first day of our visit through the hearty and sincere welcome as we passed the peace on Pentecost Sunday. Earlier in the week, a mail carrier shared bottled water with our children and me when we waved him down as he drove by and asked for directions back to the church. We were slightly lost and exhausted on a hot afternoon walk through Holy Comforter's neighborhood. He saw our lack of water as I talked to him, and he offered what he had—hospitality. That same generosity characterizes this parish; church members realized a large number of people with chronic mental illness in Atlanta were greatly underserved, imagined what offering hospitality to them might look like, and followed the way of the Holy Comforter to establish Friendship Center.

Photo: Kristin Carroccino, Church of the Holy Comforter Friendship House Art Center, Atlanta. May 2012.

This Place is Like Rehab for the Soul.
Michael

"Come on in guys, it's time for worship."

Watching Father Mike Tanner—already vested in his bright red and gold chasuble for Pentecost—open the back door of the church and call to the smokers by the picnic tables to come in for worship, I found myself reminded of the story of St. Lawrence. When asked by the emperor to bring forth "the treasures of the church," Lawrence unexpectedly brought the lame and the beggars of the city, announcing, "Behold, the treasures of the church!" With Father Mike holding the door, several men of various ages and abilities walked, hobbled, or dragged themselves up the back ramp that leads toward the nave. Welcome to the Church of the Holy Comforter in Atlanta, where the smoker's patio is only the first of many features that set this community apart from a typical Episcopal church.

"Everything changes after you spend time here."

When you ask people at Holy Comforter how the church provides for their personal spirituality, nobody mentions the usual suspects like EFM or the Sunday sermons. Instead, nearly everyone has a story to tell that reveals deep convictions. For some, Holy Comforter is a refuge, the "only place I can go" for community "where I won't be judged;" for others it is a call to action: "I don't think I would go to church if I didn't see people being helped." Whether a refuge or a spiritual boot camp, clearly no one leaves the Church of the Holy Comforter unaffected by its mission. Many marginalized people find themselves buoyed into a new life of independence and self-care, while "more mainstream" (in the parlance of the community) individuals come here to see acts of kindness that "don't happen in [their] world." One of Holy Comforter's primary forms of outreach is simply to invite volunteer groups from Atlanta to participate in their programming. A full-time program coordinator facilitates those connections.

"So many people are interested in Holy Comforter; probably because they don't think it can be done."

For the last thirty years, Holy Comforter has primarily defined itself by its outreach to people with mental illness in Atlanta, many of whom have previously been homeless. About seventy-five percent of the parish budget goes toward the Friendship Center, a day program that runs twice a week for about 120 people, offering them art classes, a gardening center, breakfast and lunch, and various other aspects of healthy community life they cannot find anywhere else. Many of them call Holy Comforter their spiritual home as well. The concept of Friendship Center started in the early 1980s when the parish was facing the possibility of closing. Parishioners looked around their neighborhood, found a group home for people with mental illness, and invited them to come and worship. From that humble beginning a completely new kind of community formed. Thirty years later, attending a vestry meeting is comparable to watching the board of directors at a nonprofit. Discussing the upcoming bishop election, there was no mention of political or ecclesial issues, only a mention of each candidate and the personal connections they made during last week's visit to the parish. The vestry directs most of its energy toward serving and maintaining the community served by Friendship Center and ensuring its services can continue well into the future.

"The main thing that holds us all together is the religious services."

The people who have experienced transformation in their lives at Holy Comforter are the first to link that transformation to the work of the Holy Spirit through the community. "Everybody tries to be the Good Samaritan here." Surprisingly, even with the bulk of their energy focused on the Friendship Center, Holy Comforter still maintains the usual outreach programs you'd find in other Episcopal churches: they've purchased several mosquito nets to help people dying of malaria in Africa and have occasionally had bake sales to raise funds. It is a parish like many others, and yet it is not: "Holy Comforter is not a viable model for the whole church." Their budget includes grant monies from a variety of sources and donations from myriad Atlanta parishes. "You look at the budget and you see these numbers, like thirty-three dollars in the bank, and you think, 'thank God for the big church, because without that—without their funds—we can't do this.'" This mission represents the collaboration of a wide variety of communities and organizations.

"It didn't matter who I was."

Cheerful openness characterized our visit to Holy Comforter. My family arrived just as the last of the Friendship Center programming was ending for the day, and we found ourselves surrounded by smiling people who were more than happy to show us around and give us directions. In almost every interview, participants mentioned the word "welcome" more than once. It seems that one of the biggest strengths that people notice about this community is its incredible hospitality. When you sit in a pew on a muggy May morning next to someone who—despite their bright smile—is wearing every stitch of winter clothing they own, appearances start to mean less. No matter where people land on the spectrum of mainstream and marginalized, each of them leave Holy Comforter feeling "a true sense of belonging," "a whole sense of forgiveness and acceptance."

"I'm trying to sing and can't find the melody—it's like being detached from reality. I started wondering: 'Is this in any way similar to the experiences of people who can't quite get a grip on reality?'"

Staff and volunteers at Holy Comforter are energetically curious about the experiences and perceptions of the marginalized population in their midst. The stories are poignant and rich: the worship music on the Sunday of our visit consisted of a small orchestra playing a Bach concerto in a fluidly inelegant tempo and tonality, and yet I can easily say that it was one of the most moving renditions I've heard. The players clearly had training and experience, and they brought their offering in full confidence, joyfully giving of their skills for the benefit of all. Sometimes the music or the prayers go awry—my sermon garnered a comment or two from the pews, hardly out of the ordinary at Holy Comforter—but always there is a sense that worship is a unifying experience for the whole community. Celebration is the heart of parish life at Holy Comforter.

Imagine a column of church vans pulling into the parking lot of an Appleby's restaurant, filled to overflowing with people who have not eaten in a restaurant for years. They get to order whatever they want; they are tired from a day of riding horses and fishing. Church of the Holy Comforter celebrated Christmas this way with Friendship Center last year. This group of people is a parish, a community, a nonprofit, a church that worships with and draws on a tremendous network of resources for a community of people living chronically on society's margins. ("If we shut down the Friendship Center, it would be a disaster for hundreds of people.") The mission of the church, according to one interviewee, is "to tell the world that God loves them. . .that witness is not just to poor people, it is to every kind of person, but it is best spoken in the context of action." Spoken off-handedly one day during our visit, a comment from Father Mike summed up what we can best learn from Holy Comforter: "churches [need to] have the experience of being vital to the lives of people."

Actions not Words. *Mike Tanner*

We don't talk much about evangelism at Holy Comforter, though we do it all the time. That may be because we have a bad taste in our mouths from experiences with evangelism that focuses narrowly on getting individuals into the church, "the ark of salvation," or getting them "saved" by "accepting Jesus as their personal savior," so that they won't be "left behind" when our Lord returns.

This is not to say that we don't believe that Jesus saves. We do. It is not to say that we don't believe that the church plays a role in God's healing of the world. We do.

We live, however, in a time when words are as cheap as they have ever been. The church bears significant responsibility for the skepticism that often greets our words about God's love for the world in Jesus Christ. We say that God loves the world, but too often behave as if God loves only us and our kind. We don't seem to make the connection between salvation and how we live in the world today.

What speaks most convincingly in our skeptical world is our loving the world as God loves the world. This loving is not talk; it is action. It is consistently putting the welfare of others, whether neighbor, stranger, or enemy, before our own welfare. While there are global manifestations of such love, it is most clearly and convincingly manifest when we risk loving the other up close, face to face.

At Holy Comforter, such love usually looks like the gracious welcome that we who live near the economic and social mainstream of society experience in the face of people marginalized by poverty and mental illness. Though we have much and they have little, they welcome us as peers. Though we have been the stigmatizers and they the stigmatized, they welcome us as friends. Though we have been the stingy and they the needy, they welcome us, and in their friendship and grace, we experience the love of the crucified, the stigmatized, the marginalized Christ.

Father Mike served as the vicar of The Episcopal Church of the Holy Comforter in Atlanta from 2008 to 2013.

Giving Thanks for Holy Trinity Parish, Decatur, Georgia. *Kristin*

The first thing I recollect seeing as we pulled into the parking lot of Holy Trinity Parish in Decatur, Georgia, was a huge array of solar panels on the roof of what I later learned was a spacious fellowship hall crowned by a beautiful stained glass window honoring children. Father Greg Tallant told us during a tour of the grounds that, remarkably, the solar panels will likely not "pay for themselves" any time soon, but the church family had elected to install them anyway for the good of the surrounding community. Energy credits generated by the panels will go back into the power grid and be an example of environmental stewardship for the neighborhood.

This generosity did not come as a surprise. We were visiting Holy Trinity to thank them for granting to Michael, me, and the *Boats without Oars* vision a Holy Trinity Centennial Scholarship. Like investing in green energy created by the solar panels for the benefit of Decatur, Georgia, providing financial resources to seminary students who are exploring ways churches can bring more life to communities demonstrates Holy Trinity's good stewardship of the gifts they have been given. This group of Episcopalians is not afraid to invest their resources faithfully and freely in projects that will not have direct, immediate impacts upon the daily workings of their parish.

During our tour of the campus, the faces of fifty-three stained glass children smiled down on us from their glassy height in the fellowship hall: a lasting memorial to the importance this parish places on children being fully functioning community members. We made our way through the buildings and gardens and preschool play areas outdoors, noticing the respect and care given to all of the church grounds. Yesterday was the last day of the church's preschool, a vibrant and accessible program offering affordable tuition for neighborhood families. An overflowing community vegetable garden skirts the playground where our own children play as we chat with Father Greg. Life is abundant around here, even on this relatively "quiet" day.

Things will be noisier this weekend when Holy Trinity celebrates Trinity Sunday. Parishioners will enjoy a barbeque lunch and dessert social following a worship service in which recipients of the Centennial Scholarship will be announced. Holy Trinity is giving wind to our sails, supporting us as we go about collecting stories and sharing them. We are thankful for their generous provision.

Church as Network. *Jonny Baker*

A metaphor I have played with is church as a network. This seems to fit with some of the writing around new ways of being and relating such as those expressed in Clay Shirky's book *Here Comes Everybody* which contains a chapter that explores networks through what is called small world theory. Here's a quick summary

If you are in a small group of friends, everyone connects to everyone else pretty easily, but it doesn't take long before that suddenly requires a huge number of connections for everyone to connect to everyone else. So what actually happens in practice is that people connect to a relatively small number of people (their small world). But as long as that small group has one or two people who also connect to people in the wider network in another small group, it's only one step removed to reach anyone else in the network through the connector. This is how most networks work—a mix of dense and sparse connections rather than everyone linked to everyone. These people who focus externally are connectors. Most people are quite happy existing in a small world, but connectors often hold an astonishing level of connectivity across small worlds. Six degrees of separation works because these people create huge short-cuts, and it's often these connectors that people start thinking about unconsciously when looking for that connection in a conversation to establish common ground.

So imagine a group of five small Christian communities. Now there is no way that everyone in each of those groups will connect to everyone else in the other groups and why would they? But with one or two connectors, the insights/gifts flow round the whole network just as well or have the potential to do so and this really is a microcosm—if we really mapped the connections in the church and started adding all the creative connections it would be unbelievable to think what gifts and connections there are. In [terms of] mission the former Church Mission Society (CMS) general secretary Max Warren called this "interchange," which is rather a lovely way of describing this process.

The obvious rider to this is that some groups don't necessarily have natural external connectors and I know groups who think external connections are a waste of time altogether. But the benefit you'll gain by encouraging someone(s) to focus externally will be huge so it's worth thinking about, even though most people remain locally focused. Shirky calls these two types of relating bonding and bridging capital. How much of each do the key small worlds you are in have? Is it a good balance?

One of the interesting sections in Clay Shirky's chapter is a story of a firm that had new management and a piece of research done to see which managers came up with the most creative solutions. The discovery was that those that were least locked into their own department brought the most creativity (i.e. lots of their connections were external). As he put it: bridging capital puts people at greater risk of having good ideas. In any network, there is a balance to be had. The temptation is to want to keep it tight—i.e. relate to people with similar passions/interests etc., as you share concerns, struggles, etc. But the network will stifle if it is too tight—it needs random elements and connections that are totally different to bring a creative edge.

The network of Christ is a global mission network of small worlds and connectors. We only really know who Jesus is as we see Christ's many faces, theological takes, and gifts round the global body/network/multitude of Christ. But we need to be intentional about connecting with difference rather than just sameness so there can be an interchange. The tragedy of the network of Christ is that we seem to be following the opposite instinct and gathering together with people who mirror our own theological takes!

Social media tools mean we are relating in small worlds and connectors all the time without even thinking about it, and the scale of networking response/influence can be on a huge scale when things start to flow. None of us can really control the network and we are all severely limited in our relational capacity (or monkey sphere as it's known in the theory!), so we only ever see a part of the whole—we can simply participate and get in the flow as it were. . .

Riffing on this metaphor of the network of Christ, I have had a go at an improvised reworking of 1 Corinthians 12:12-end.

> ### The Network of Christ:
> *Just as a network, though one, has many small worlds, but all its parts interconnect, so it is with Christ. For we were all baptized by one Spirit and given a portal into the wider network of Christ—whether Orthodox, Emerging, Missional, New Monastic, Catholic, Anglican, Post-denominational, Pentecostal, Baptist, Anabaptist etc., or any blend of the above the Spirit flows through our networks. So, the network of Christ is not made up of one small world but of many interconnected small worlds and hubs.*
>
> *If the Australian missional communities should say, "because I am not focused on worship I don't connect into the wider network," it would not*

cease to be part of the global network of Christ. And, if the French Catholic church should say, "because I can't feasibly imagine homogeneous missional church planting, I don't belong to the wider network," it wouldn't cease to be part of the global network of Christ either. If the whole network lived in the small world of Alternative Worship, where would the growth of African churches be? If the whole network lived in the Anglican small world, where would the prophetic passion for justice of the Anabaptists be? But, in fact, in the network of Christ, God has catalyzed and flows in lots of small worlds, just as God wills. And, the network is such that the Spirit creates an environment where She flows, and small worlds emerge as the Spirit beckons the network into the future.

If there were just one small world with no external connectors, where would the network be? The redemptive gifts that the Spirit has distributed throughout the wider network of Christ would not flow. They would remain static. So, don't let the small world of which you are a part ever say, "I don't need you" to another small world, and don't despise the gift of external connection. To be in Christ is to connect to Christ and to participate in the Network of Christ where the Spirit flows.

And, be careful that you don't just notice the hubs that seem important or powerful or branded, and neglect the weaker or less connected small worlds. God flows in these parts, distributes gifts there, and has a special love for them. And, the small world in which you mostly participate is most likely to be energized by connection to other small worlds which are the most different to you, so don't be tempted to just connect to others who seem like you.

You are the network of Christ, and each one of you is connected and participates. And, the Spirit flows in and through you, and has distributed different kinds of gifts and roles—pioneers, catalysts, networkers, artists, mission leaders, loyal radicals, local practitioners, environmentalists, all guardians of flow. Are all external connectors? Are all local practitioners? But, eagerly desire the greater gifts to flow throughout the network of Christ.

Jonny is part of the Church Mission Society in England and a voice in the emerging church movement there. He put this post together from a couple of previous posts on his blog: "The Network of Christ" and "It's a Small World." You can read more of his writing on his blog: jonnybaker.blogs.com.

We Must Allow Ourselves to be Transformed.
Jeremiah Griffin

"If my people who are called by my name humble themselves, pray, seek my face, and turn from their wicked ways, then I will hear from heaven, and will forgive their sin and heal their land" (2 Chronicles 7:14).

The other day, I heard a story on National Public Radio of a former minister who lost her faith. She left her congregation and immediately joined a local group for atheists in her town. Standing before this new assembly, she spoke of her past profession and life's journey, saying, "I was the one on the right track, and you were the ones that were going to burn in hell…and I'm happy to say as I stand before you right now, I'm going to burn with you."

Her story, while notable because she was a minister, is one that's all too familiar these days. It seems something in the water is causing people to lose their faith. Perhaps I'm reading into things, but I have to wonder if her thinly construed statement about hell gives us a clue as to what drove her away? Could it be that she found herself boxed in by bad theology and saw no way out? Or maybe she had come to see the church as a bunch of self-righteous, inflexible ideologues. While I'm not opposed to people leaving faiths they find toxic or unhelpful, I am saddened when people leave unnecessarily.

Perhaps her departure came after years of frustration of being associated with a religion known for pushing inane, Armageddon-focused book series, Creationism in schools, and corrupt political leaders claiming to support Christian values. Recent decades have left our faith tarred and feathered in the eyes of many. When people hear "Christian," lots think of angry, hypocritical, materialistic people, who have resisted the fair treatment of women, the findings of modern science, and any number of other sensible ideas. It's no wonder that recent studies found the fastest growing faith affiliation in the U.S. to be "none."

For those of us who've stuck around, who truly believe in the church's life-giving, transformative message, if we hope to reach out to rising generations, we need to recognize that a new posture is in order. The combative, dogmatic tenor of yesteryear causes younger generations to bristle. Similarly, passionless and milquetoast presentations of the Gospel only inspire yawns. What's needed is a hospitable, convicted body of believers, so smitten with their Divine Lover that they can't help but take on His attributes of generosity, peacemaking, and reconciliatory healing. Sounds great, right? But where can we find that?

First, we pray. The church is, after all, called to be the priest of the new covenant. We are to intercede for a bleeding planet in desperate need of salvation. We must do so as individuals, but also collectively. Then, we wait on the Lord.

I can't speak for others, but when I quiet myself before God…things change. I change. My actions change. I learn how to listen and see others with compassion. Both conviction and inspiration seep into me, each of them slowly working on my stubbornness, pride, and selfish ambition, and each time leaving me a little more "God-shaped." Morning after morning, when I pray the words of the Daily Office, its tendrils of scripture and prayer coil themselves around me, covering over preoccupations that would keep me from striving to glorify God.

I mention all this because I have learned that we must allow ourselves to be transformed, before God will use us to transform others. Then, we must listen for God's leading and trust that whatever needs to happen will happen. If creative measures emerge or new liturgies are sung into being, they will be of God's doing…and not our own. If homes are mended, gardens are planted, and communities restored, it will be the work of the Spirit that guides us.

For now, let us focus on allowing God to draw us ever-deeper into His love by sinking our roots downwards into the rich sands of past revelation. There, we can draw nourishment for today's life and tomorrow's blossoming. Our new posture can be one of clinging tightly to the tradition passed down to us, yet doing so with humility, always acknowledging the incomplete nature of our vision. Let us welcome the doubters, those struggling to see any grace left in humanity, and those convinced they have no need to listen to others…for those people are us all. Let us repent of past arrogances, divisive infighting, and complacency, opening our hearts to God and one another. Then, and only then, will we have something compelling to share with those tempted to fall away from their faith. Then, and only then, will we begin to see the in-breaking of God's Kingdom, spreading like fire through the hearts of a new generation.

Jeremiah is a priest serving at Trinity Episcopal Church in Galveston, Texas, and as the Executive Director of the William Temple Episcopal Center, a student ministry of the Episcopal Diocese of Texas. He is passionate about matters concerning ecology and faith, and spends much of his free time exploring nearby coastal lands with his family.

Interview with Becky Garrison. *Kristin*

We met Becky Garrison a few months ago at a book signing sponsored by St. Hildegard's Community in Austin, Texas, for her 2011 publication Ancient Future Disciples: Meeting Jesus in Mission-Shaped Ministries. *Following that, we began a conversation about* Boats without Oars *and Becky's reflections on the parishes she studied while writing her book. She graciously accepted our request to share some follow-up thoughts from her study.*

Kristin: "What do you see as a unifying issue or core value among the Episcopal churches you've studied—those that embrace change and the neighbors around them?"

Becky: The core value I keep finding in these communities is what I call "radical inclusivity." During an e-mail interview with Tripp York over at the Amish Jihadist[14], I break down what I mean by this phrase. I use this term to reference those churches who try to live out the baptismal covenant whereby one welcomes "all." This means you have a church governed not by political correctness to the left or a set of rigid doctrinal statements on the right, but a real push to "try" and put the Greatest Commandment into practice (Matt. 22:36-40). In these communities, one finds diversity in gender, sexual orientation, ethnicities, and political leanings. They've moved well beyond these ongoing conversations one finds in even progressive evangelical circles, where one may "talk" about affirming women and LGBT people, but their leadership remains dominated by white men who self-identify as straight. Instead, one finds LGBT folks, women, and people of color at all levels of leadership. Your call which picture more accurately represents the Kingdom of God.

In my conversation about my book *Ancient Future Disciples* with Greg Garrett,[15] I offered these observations about what I found during my travels. While the communities I studied are informed by their particular cultural context, some identifying markers they share in common began to emerge:

† The vast majority of these ministries started with little or no money, and those with money had scant institutional backing.

---

[14] "[Tripp York] Five Questions with Becky Garrison," May 6, 2012. *www.profligategrace.com/?p=776.*
[15] "Greg Garrett: Ancient Future Disciples: A Q&A with Becky Garrison." January 21, 2012. *http://day1.org/3568-greg_garrett_ancient_future_disciples_a_qa_with_becky_garrison.*

† These ministries were more likely to succeed when a bishop either supported them or adopted a Gamaliel approach (Acts 5:34-39) to leave the endeavor alone as long as it did no harm.

† These ministries needed to be free from the pressure to produce results quickly, as it takes time and space to develop a viable community.

† Those starting the ministry have entrepreneurial mindsets, who are going to do this ministry whether or not they have denominational backing. These risk takers felt called to reach out beyond their comfort zone and venture toward where they felt the Holy Spirit was calling them.

† Following Jesus tends to trump particular political ideology. And so, you will often find diversity of political viewpoints among those who frequent these ministries. When they take a stand on a political issue such as immigration, sex trafficking, or equality legislation, it is because the cause resonates with their understanding of what it means to live out the teachings of Jesus.

† These leaders place a high value on the people's engagement and empowerment, not only in worship, but in the whole ministry. They help spiritual seekers to discern what kind of community they want to create together. Here the leader functions more like a DJ or curator who is working behind the scenes instead of being front and center.

† The U.S.-based ministries are often led by women, a notable proportion of them women of color. Also, one finds LGBT people involved in all aspects of leadership. The communities also tend to be more racially inclusive, intergenerational, and affirming than the traditional mainline congregation.

Also, in talking with fellow reporter, Eileen Flynn,[16] we talked about those who have left behind what I termed unbiblical BS. I noted I sense that a number of spiritual seekers would find space to reflect, play, and explore questions in many of the communities I keep discovering in my travels. Just call it a strong hunch.

Becky's writing credits include work for The Guardian, Killing the Buddha, American Atheist Magazine, Perceptive Travel, Religion Dispatches, The Revealer, Geez Magazine, US Catholic, *and the now defunct* Wittenburg Door. *When she takes a break from her laptop, Becky can often be found kayaking, fly-fishing, biking, or hiking.*

---

[16] "Q&A: Author Becky Garrison talks mission-shaped ministries and unbiblical BS." November 17, 2011. *http://eileenflynn.wordpress.com/2011/11/17/qa-author-becky-garrison-talks-mission-shaped-ministries-and-unbiblical-bs/*.

Inside Outside. *Rebecca Hall*

The church likes to profess that it is the only institution that exists for the benefit of those not yet its members. Is this really true? Where we place our attention (both in our personal and corporate lives) becomes reality. And the Episcopal Church's attention tends to primarily focus inward, even in thriving communities, with excellent worship, outreach, and formation. All good things, mind you. Things toward which I put most of my time and energy as a church staff person.

But, last fall, six of us at St. David's (a large, thriving, church in downtown Austin, Texas) began the program "Called Back to the Well." The purpose was to teach church leadership how to inject spirituality into parish life. This program was not about evangelism; yet quite by accident last December, our team found itself passionate about communicating the church's Advent message to Austin's downtown community. We took the Bible phrase, "The word became flesh and dwelt among us" and pondered how we could express that in a way to engage the hundreds of people who park in our parking garage and walk by our building, but do not set foot inside the doors of the church. Since Advent is about God interrupting, coming into our lives in surprising and unexpected ways, we decided to graffiti the retaining wall of our church with, "Light Is Home In You." We called our project Light Interrupts and set up a blog with the same name.[17] Each week for the four weeks of Advent, we painted a new message on the wall, all pointing to God working in surprising ways in our lives. Yes, our church graffitied its own retaining wall. This interrupted everyone's lives—we made the news, our vestry was divided, some church members wanted it gone, and the police showed up and handcuffed the teenager we had commissioned to do the graffiti. But, mostly people loved it. The blog got 6,000 hits. And people posted and reposted pictures of it on Facebook and Twitter, saying, "Look what MY church did!"

---

[17] Blog address: www.lightinterrupts.org

Now we're starting an Easter project, and we've begun in the same way. We took the phrase "Christ Is Risen," and thought about how to communicate that to St. David's and non-St. David's folks. This Easter project is called "Do Not Be Afraid. New Life Happens." In the next two weeks. we're going to stencil this on the wall, along with the web address newlifehappens.org. The site will invite people to look for where New Life is happening in their lives and take a picture of it, send it in, and we'll post it. In the end, we hope to have a large collection of examples of New Life in the world.

So, at St. David's we have shifted just a little bit. We have begun to put some attention, for some of us a significant amount of attention, toward the spiritual formation of those not already in our community. This second project launches next week on May 13, and it is our hope that it will help people—all people who see it from parishioners to the busy downtown worker—to stop and notice this essential message. Do not be afraid. New life happens.

Rebecca is the Director of Adult Christian Education and Spiritual Formation at St. David's Episcopal Church and a Master in Spiritual Formation student at Seminary of the Southwest. Her passion is figuring out how to help people (both Christian and "spiritual-but-not-religious") grow spiritually and become more aware of God in their lives.

St. David's graffiti image from the Diocese of Texas website:
http://www.epicenter.org/article/st-davids-austin-welcomes-advent-with-graffiti/

"Graffiti is the New Red Door." Conversation with David Boyd, Rector of St. David's Episcopal Church, Austin, Texas. *Kristin and Michael*

Father David Boyd may be found anywhere at any given time during his working hours at St. David's Episcopal Church in downtown Austin. I've seen him on Sunday mornings greeting the stream of visitors and members flowing in the doors between services with a smile and firm handshake. He drops by to check in with groups of women during their "Friday Morning Moms" meetings, kneels down to talk to a few children at the recent "Children's Stations of the Cross" on Good Friday, or stops in at the Trinity Center, a hub providing spiritual, emotional, and physical care for people experiencing poverty located in the basement of St. David's, which is situated across from one of the city's largest homeless shelters. In his ninth year of serving as rector of Austin's largest Episcopal church, Fr. David is undoubtedly busy, but he doesn't present as an anxious person or seem distracted when he stops to greet someone and pat them on the back.

In fact, Fr. David's gaze is deep and intent, and it's obvious that he has a deep care and concern for all who enter the doors of his parish. A few weeks ago, we had the opportunity to interview Fr. David as part of our *Boats without Oars* research, a warm-up for all of the summer interviews. He greeted us in the lobby and guided us back to his office, a comfortable distance from both the nave and the bustle of other staff members. A pair of cowboy boots stood at the ready by the door. Perhaps he would change into them later for his ride home through the streets of downtown on his black scooter. A lit candle marked our time as sacred.

With a touch of iconoclasm, Fr. David envisions a modern reclamation of an ancient faith. He does not use Rite I at any of his services, and has been known to move worship services to other rooms from time to time in order to accommodate other (paying) functions in the church building. He says, "If the Episcopal Church doesn't change significantly, it's going to die" and he sees much of his ministry as figuring out what that significant change looks like. "Churches need to be more multidimensional," meaning that "church" might begin to happen in more unexpected places—such as houses and storefronts—and use more informal liturgies. He charges that Episcopalians can no longer be "the beautiful people...coming to church for their hour with God." Instead, we have to be ready to embrace even the kind of people who are "going to cost us," invite them to discipleship, and send them out the door to do the work of the church.

"When I was ordained almost thirty years ago, all you had to do was paint the door red and people would come. Ever since then, things have gotten leaner and leaner and leaner." Fr. David spoke frankly about economic needs and circumstances both across the church and in his own parish, and the inevitable end toward which they lead. Innovation, then, is the order of the day, and St. David's doesn't shy away from it. Fr. David says the church was already primed for innovation when he came, with no serious scandal or upset since the 1930s and a historically strong cohort of young people. In his tenure, he has done everything in his power to "make the walls of the church more permeable," including putting graffiti on them! "We should always keep a list of about ten things we want to try, and see how they turn out. If two or three of them work, that's a success." "I'm a coward and I'm afraid, but I want to be faithful. Very few of these ideas have been mine," he says, "but I see my role as being to give permission. I cannot claim strong leadership, but listening to the Spirit of God." When we asked Fr. David about the metaphor "boats without oars" and if it represents St. David's, he responded, "The wind of the Spirit has shaped us. There has been a clear direction to say 'yes' at uncertain times. I want to hoist a big sail to capture more of the Spirit's guidance."

Fr. David sees the church as a spiritual resource for the whole of downtown Austin. "Every soul is welcome," and the primary focus—and success—of his ministry is "the deepening of souls." He imagines St. David's along the lines of the ancient model of cathedrals: a center for light and learning and resources for the care of souls. Attendance patterns and approaches to spirituality are changing for younger generations, and St. David's is making itself available to people of all different ages and backgrounds in a variety of ways. That openness attracts new people. "Since we can't just paint the door red, what we can do is be faithful with what God has given us."

Our time with Fr. David passed quickly. He is direct, intense, and thoughtful, very engaging. Our meeting ended with him asking pointed questions and expressing care and concern over our individual callings and our children's well-being over the course of the summer, then sent us on our way with traveling mercies before blowing out the candle and walking back with us through the corridors of this large, thriving parish. A few people are drinking lattes in the bookstore as we pass, and a few more are standing by the edge of the outdoor labyrinth. As we exit the building, we pass by several visitors and a staff member who have walked upstairs from the Trinity Center. We depart via the adjacent parking garage, which serves as parking for the many Sunday and Wednesday worshippers, and is a source of income for the parish during the workweek and during Austin's famously large music and arts festivals. St. David's is a church and Fr. David a leader that are open to the future, already hoisting a large sail and following the wind of the Spirit.

Image from the public domain. Irish curagh.

Reverse Evangelism. *Terry Pierce*

I was confirmed in the Episcopal Church at the age of forty-six. Five years later, I moved to Austin suffering from severe depression. I made little effort to find a church. At a retreat sponsored by a Sufi community in Austin, I learned a simple method of contemplative prayer called remembrance, which is to sit with a string of beads and repeat or remember the name of God, Allah, at each bead. I began to pray with that community and later accepted a job as accountant for the community.

I learned to pray five times each day at the time that all Muslims are praying and I learned politeness, *adab*. The inner politeness is how I present myself and am present with Allah; it is to be in the deepest humility and surrender to God. The outer politeness is how I present myself and am present in the world. On the outer, *adab* is to prostrate myself in prayer, my forehead pressed to the earth. In politeness, I wash myself before I pray; whether man or woman, I am modest in my dress and cover my head and form to pray; and I am modest in my language and response towards other people. I recognize that everything is God and I respond to everything from that recognition—that is what it means to be in the *adab*.

This community called my name as precious beloved of God and taught me to call to God as I would to my beloved. They taught me to be polite, to listen and to be obedient, and to value those things as expectations of how I am to interact with all of God's creation. They showed me what it was to live a religious practice in community on a daily basis, to be received in community in my brokenness and imperfection, and to experience God's love through the community. In Sufi practices, my sense of God as transcendent, all-powerful, mysterious, and unknowable is heightened by the beauty of the language, by radical obedience to a schedule that demands my presence when it demands my presence, by the disappearance of my form beneath a covering of robes and veils, and by the prostration of my body and the bowing of my face to the earth.

Reverence in that community for the prophet Isa, Jesus, led me into a new relationship as believer, beloved, and servant of Jesus, the Christ. In understanding what this community believed Jesus was not, I understood that I was called to proclaim what I believe he is. I could name Jesus, incomparably divine and brokenly human, Son of God who is God. This Sufi community showed me how to worship God and how to incorporate spiritual practice as a way of daily living. My relationships with them led me to reclaim my place in the Christian community with a new understanding of what it is to worship in every breath and to proclaim Jesus Christ Lord "not only with our lips, but in our lives."

Terry Pierce is the Pastoral Leader of St. James Episcopal Church in Taylor, Texas.

The Episcopal Evangelism Network. *Carol Morehead*

When I first started seminary, I was intrigued by an e-mail about an interseminary organization called the Episcopal Evangelism Network (EEN) and a seminar they were hosting in Baltimore. I pursued it with the faculty, and before I knew it, I was winging my way on a plane to Maryland, where I met a group of seminarians from other places, none of whom I knew. Members of the Cathedral in Baltimore generously opened their homes, offering us places to stay through the Episco-Couch program. Happily, I ended up with a real bed and wonderful hosts. That early seminar offered me an entry into EEN, and I learned that wonderful things were happening within our church, things I had not yet heard about. The Good News of God in Christ was being proclaimed in big and small ways, in cities and counties, in ways that sometimes looked a little different.

There were people dancing at the altar, singing new songs, exploring ways that God is at work in their communities. It was inspiring, and I was excited to share God with others. When I returned to Seminary of the Southwest, I began a local chapter along with other interested students. Part of the mission of EEN is to help seminarians engage evangelism in an Episcopal way, because *for many of us, evangelism is kind of a dirty word*. So, we wanted to reclaim it. Through EEN, local chapters are able to explore what evangelism would look like for us, how to actually engage others in conversations about God, how to form community from the diverse people who come together seeking Christ.

Fast forward to the spring of 2012, and the various chapters of EEN worked together to put on a Missional Development Conference, with the dream of seeing the vision of EEN expanded beyond seminaries to the larger church. Together with bishops, canons, priests, and church leaders, our little band of seminarians led all participants through a creative process of visioning, dreaming, and planning, with the hope that perhaps we could bring together a coalition of people who shared the vision of doing evangelism, Episcopal style. Through the gracious support and facilities of Trinity Church in New York, we gathered leaders, and what followed was truly amazing. God's Spirit was at work, in conversations and brainstorming, in worship and prayer, as we imagined a new way to share God's saving and reconciling power through the church in new and perhaps uncharted ways. The assembled group talked about so many aspects: What kinds of people are called to this specific ministry? How does the church support them, or at times fail to support them? How can seminaries include more evangelism in the curriculum? And is that even the best, or the only way to train evangelists and entrepreneurial leaders? What resources does the church have to bring to such a coalition? What other church organizations can help with this vision through resources and work they are already doing?

After praying together, singing together, dreaming on post-it notes and poster boards, we realized that we were, in fact, witnesses to the birth of a new work of God. And I was truly stuck by the deep faith and love that I saw in every person there, love for a hurting world, faith in God's justice, belief that we are called to be God's presence to our communities through our church. There was a palpable yearning to reach out, to be open to where the Spirit is leading. The conference culminated with generous gifts of support in order to see where this new life will lead, and the formation of an exploratory committee who are busy at work to bring this vision to life.

In the weeks that have followed, the exploratory committee has been meeting. Their work on the specific way this new coalition can work and interact with the broader church is ongoing. This is really happening! Praise God that a few seminarians scattered around the country have connected with those who are on the ground, doing evangelism in very intentional and specific ways, and together we are forging new ground in our church for God's reign. Stay tuned...

Carol is the associate rector at St. Mark's Episcopal Church in San Antonio, Texas. She shares her life with her husband, three sons, two dogs, and two cats. Their house has a lot of pizza, jazz, laughter, and Led Zeppelin, plus volumes and volumes of books, mostly about God and kung fu.

Questions

How have you experienced conversion in your life of faith?

Are specific people "called" to evangelism?

Does evangelism mean actions? Words? Both?

Is evangelism limited to the Christian faith?

When, if ever, is it okay for a church to "die"?

JUNE 2012: CHASING SUMMER NORTH

We have driven east from Texas, across the Deep South, and slightly north. We have begun our ascent up the eastern seaboard after camping for a week in northern Georgia. There, we searched for fool's gold in swift mountain creeks and took the kids on a hike to the waterfall along the Appalachian Trail where Michael and I exchanged wedding vows twelve years earlier.

We have visited many churches, some part of the formal *Boats without Oars* study, and others not, just beautiful or compelling in their own right. Our children have grown accustomed to church nurseries and friendly church people, sometimes surly in their requests for "more macaroni and cheese!" or extra animal crackers during Sunday school story time. In one hotel in northern Virginia, Mirella, accustomed to utilizing so many public restrooms, looked in vain for the electronic hand dryer on the wall before realizing towels are more customary in motor lodges. Caedmon is no longer afraid of escalators.

We have chased fireflies on the National Mall, stood on the hill where the Wright Brothers launched their first successful airplane flight, eaten many sandwiches while driving, visited farmers' markets and received free gifts of pickling cucumbers for snacks. We have watched the seasons change as we move up the U.S. map from spring to summer. With every couple of states we travel north, it seems that new pairs of birds are building their first spring nests. Fields turn from grassy green to a panoply of vivid wildflowers. We have grilled corn on our camp stove on an isolated stretch of the Outer Banks, only to be driven away by a sudden thunderstorm blowing sheets of sand as unwelcome garnish to our meal. I spend time every day writing in my journal and taking photos. We read books aloud about church growth and storytelling. We listen to books read aloud by others on the car stereo. Roald Dahl and Beatrix Potter are current favorites. And always there is music and the hope of a campfire for s'mores in the evening, or a home-cooked meal at a parishioner's house. The travel and the growing and learning are sweet indeed.

—Kristin

Christian symbol of the church as a ship. Artist Rudolf Koch. Source: public domain.

"They Felt Welcomed, I Think."
Michael

One word that seems to come up frequently when I talk to parishioners about church is "welcome." People obsess about how "welcoming" their church is, the experience of first-time guests, the quality of their community's hospitality, their restrooms, their coffee, etc. I have seen the word "Welcome!" on countless church signs of numerous denominations as we have driven across the lower half of the United States. Apparently, "welcome" somehow strikes at the heart of what it is that people think the church should be about. Ultimately, the sheer frequency of sighting the word on church signs proves them right, but I wonder how much thought goes into the use of the word. What does welcome really mean?

We visited Old Donation Episcopal Church in Virginia Beach, Virginia, for Sunday worship during our week off from doing interviews (Decatur and Atlanta are now checked off the list; we have five more churches to go), and we were delighted to discover that we had stumbled upon a special outdoor service and church picnic for Trinity Sunday. In this part of the world, the "outdoor" that surrounds most churches is populated by granite monuments, and so we sat among the headstones and statuary in our folding chairs, sang hymns, and took communion. It was an ancient Christian tradition made new. Old Donation used to hold their outdoor service on the other side of the building, but the sun was just too hot, so they moved the event to the tree-filled graveyard instead. After the service, Kristin and I had a nice discussion with Old Donation's rector, Bob Randall, as we picked our way across the cemetery toward the food.

Fr. Bob attributes years of steady church growth in his parish to clarifying the laity's role as evangelists. I hope to hear more from him about this, but it seems the quick implication is simply that he encourages the members of Old Donation to tell others about their church. There is rarely a service without visitors in attendance. Developing a practice of inviting acquaintances to church is Fr. Bob's primary answer to why this church is bucking the usual trends.

My experience during the Sunday service at Old Donation was not profoundly different from any other church to which I've been this summer. I think my Pastoral Theology professor Kathleen Russell put it well when she said, "people don't come to church for the programming, they come because they've made a connection with other people there." So welcoming, then, seems to be less about the hospitality provided in worship than the hospitality given in the weekday lives of the parishioners. Maybe the elusive and all-important "welcome" that populates so many of my conversations this summer really doesn't have an institutional face (which is not to say that greeters are not important!); it is, rather, the cultivation of hospitality in each of the members of a community. Perhaps welcoming churches are those whose members live lives of invitation.

I think if you asked people on the street what they think when they see, "all are welcome" on a church sign, you would get as many answers as people who were asked. At the very least—and this is perhaps what Episcopalians do best of all—it means that no one will be turned away, that everyone has a place at the table and a voice in the conversation. My family was turned away from a state park today as we searched for a restroom for an emergent situation in the back seat: "you have to pay the fee ($24 in our case) to come into the park and use our bathroom." This is the very opposite of welcome; we were sent away without help or compassion. Jesus, on the other hand, said, "I was a stranger and you welcomed me," and this is what we have experienced in our travels visiting churches this summer. We've gotten showered with meals and lodging and blessings just by showing up. And every time I express my gratitude, people always offer the same response: "you're welcome."

Photo: Kristin Carroccino. Churchyard at Ola Donation Church, Virginia Beach, Virginia, just after the church service ended. June 2012.

A Sense of Place: Christ Church on Capitol Hill, Washington, D.C. *Kristin*

We had been driving for two days across southern and central Virginia on a spontaneous and almost manic (on my part) quest to visit all of the oldest Episcopal churches possible in a very finite amount of time with two mostly happy and compliant children, and a husband sometimes game for my micro-obsession. Signs proclaiming one historic feat, person, or location spring out of street corners in this territory like gangly dandelions competing for a ray of sun. We speed by so many historical markers so quickly, I fret over which essential facts I'm neglecting to share with my children. I am under the delusion that standing where one brave soul or another had invented the first machine, or fired the last shot, or made the loudest proclamation might somehow inform me, in that moment, the secret of the universe. When it came to "firsts" and Anglican churches, which of course were the forebears of modern Episcopal churches, I quickly realized that one has several options when deciding on the location of the "first Episcopal church in the U.S." Wikipedia isn't even authoritative in this case, and trust me, I looked!

First, Fort Raleigh, and the "Lost Colony" of Roanoke. No sign announces that this is the location of the first meeting of Anglicans on what we now call American soil, yet I did almost pass right by a marker denoting the first known baptism of an English person in the "failed" colony—that of infant Virginia Dare. Next was Jamestown, where the ruins of at least four churches have been unearthed; the most recent archeological research reveals the church where John Rolfe and Pocahontas were married. Then, Williamsburg and Bruton Parish, the oldest continuously attended parish in the U.S., where one can sit where George Washington did so many Sundays ago.

By the end of my search, I felt enlightened though, quite frankly, tired. Everyone in the car was ready to get to the site of our third parish study, Christ Church on Capitol Hill in Washington, D.C., another important church in Episcopalian history; it is the oldest in the District. Though the stories from Christ Church's history are interesting, it's the new life springing up at the church that drew our attention. The community's regard of and respect for children attracted us when deciding which churches to study this summer.

We rolled into the parking lot laden with freshly bought groceries, which don't fit anywhere other than in laps or underfoot at this point in our saga. In fact our Camry is a modern prairie schooner chock-full of an entire household billowing down the Interstate on four reliable tires, now that one was patched back near Virginia Beach after ingesting an unfortunate bolt.

Our first welcome at Christ Church was from a little girl close in age to our daughter, whose face lit up immediately at the prospect of a playmate after several weeks of being on the road and listening to far too many grown-ups. The new friend immediately escorted our children from the gardens behind the church to the parish hall, where a room full of toys awaited my eager progeny. On a Thursday afternoon, the church was beginning to gather; many middle-aged people were getting the front lawn ready for the season's first Grill & Chill, complete with picnic fare and water toys on the front lawn. The whole neighborhood is invited.

After going through our unpacking routine, Michael and I went searching for our children in the parish hall and learned that the action had moved to the front lawn to accommodate a community children's Tae Kwan Do class that uses the space weekly. Before

Photo: Kristin Carroccino. "Grill & Chill," Christ Church on Capitol Hill. June 2012.

joining everyone else on the lawn, I stopped to read the bulletin boards and learned that a neighborhood co-op preschool uses the same space several mornings each week, and a monthly evening worship service designed for children is offered tomorrow night. Though this is a small parish, children here play a big role, whether or not they attend Sunday services.

Outside, people are cheerful and welcoming. They love being together and are excited about the new inflatable water slide for the Grill & Chills. People of all ages are here, from octogenarians to caregivers of the children playing in the water and stealing potato chips and brownies. After I load my plate with barbeque fare and look for a place to sit, I spot my daughter on her second round of food and walk over to join her at a table. We are sitting for a few moments; when I notice something I honestly think I've never seen: adults standing and offering their seats at the table to children. This is clearly not something I can remember experiencing. In fact, the opposite scenario is usually true, with grown-ups telling the kids to find a seat on the ground nearby or stand while eating next to them. I suddenly realize that this norm is one of the subtle ways which our society typically marginalizes children. Christ Church is countercultural.

After the meal, adjunct priest Betsy Gonzales and Rector Cara Spaccarelli (both mothers of preschool-aged children) gather the group of around fifteen kids and their caregivers and offer up a time of singing a few rounds of "Father Abraham" and "My God is so Great!" Then, they share a short lesson about God and being honest, which ends with the distribution of doughnut holes, much to the children's delight. While chatting with Reverends Betsy and Cara later, I learn how Christ Church seeks to welcome children by stewarding time and space in this neighborhood where lawns are scarce, by offering the front lawn as a play yard on Thursday evenings. The church also maintains a collection of toys inside the parish hall for kids to play with during the monthly Sunday evening "Play and Worship" gatherings. Christ Church has paid attention to the surrounding neighborhood, which is comprised of a growing number of families with young children, and is practicing evangelism by seeking to meet the needs of the local community.

After a week that began with chasing the history of the Episcopal Church in America across southern Virginia, I realize that at Christ Church, I am gaining more of an education. This community was once facing a significant decline in membership; they have revitalized by becoming a more integral part of their neighborhood and restructured how the church operates in relation to the least-of-these in their midst. They are living evangelism.

Photo credit: Kristin Carroccino. Rev. Cara Spacarelli instructs children and their caregivers about the Eucharist. June 2012.

"We're Trying to be a Front Porch Parish." *Michael*

My first experience of Christ Church on Capitol Hill was as a guest at their weekly summer Grill & Chill, an event that is a great example of the kind of vision this church has lately developed for its presence in a close-knit and historic neighborhood right in the heart of Washington, D.C. Among the people I interviewed, the estimates varied from eighty-five to ninety-five as to the percentage of parishioners who could walk to church on a given Sunday. It is quite clear that Christ Church is a neighborhood church in the fullest sense of the word.

Parishioners here relish that identity: with two other Episcopal churches sharing the same square mile—and a host of other options as well—this group has chosen their church because it fits the character of a place they love. Christ Church occupies the geographical center of a block hemmed in on four sides by densely packed housing, and the rectory is literally attached to the church building (Cara, the rector, can walk right out of her laundry room and into the sacristy!) The building is well designed to be the geographical anchor that it has become for the neighborhood. Because of this identity, Christ Church's makeup changes with its surroundings. One member described the parish as "chameleon-like."

In our interview with her, Rev. Cara honed the parish's identity as a neighborhood church: the people of Christ Church view their affiliation with the church as a commitment to their neighborhood, even though on Capitol Hill, they have many other virtuous organizations that could benefit from their resources. The fact that attendees choose participation in their religious community to demonstrate care of the neighborhood speaks of a deeper spiritual understanding of the essential nature of community. When asked about the mission of the church, people at Christ Church overwhelmingly tended toward answers like "to worship God" (and, of course, "to create community") more so than any parish we have visited. (Just for comparison: Holy Comforter's answers trended more toward personal transformation.) People here love community, but they also love liturgy: this parish has some of the most actively engaged worship planners I've encountered.

Parishioners here understand the history and ritual of the Eucharist and the cosmic importance of prayer to a high degree, and they plan and discuss it well. As I've reflected on this understanding of ritual in the community, it brings to mind Frank Waters' *The Book of the Hopi*, in which one Hopi elder proclaimed that their tribe was performing the rites and prayers that brought rain—and life—to the whole rest of the world. The Hopi keep doing what they do because that's who they are, and the same could be said for the people of Christ Church. Beyond these deep commitments to prayer and neighbors, people in this parish "don't want a niche."

I was in this community for a few days before I learned that Christ Church is actually the oldest church in Washington, D.C. Unlike so many historic churches I've visited, the past was not the first impression I had of Christ Church. Parishioners speak more of the present than of their church's roots, but they are still proud of its history. Thomas Jefferson attended services at this church, which had its original home in a tobacco barn, and Christ Church has seen its share of congressional representatives and famous people (John Philip Sousa was mentioned once or twice). There has also been upheaval and change. After Martin Luther King, Jr., was assassinated in 1968, riots literally tore the neighborhood apart, and a few days later Christ Church's people led their Palm Sunday procession right over the bricks and broken glass in the street.

Since those riots, a wide variety of people have been part of the community: hippies took up residence in the rectory for a time, a less-than-stellar school district kept young families away for the last few decades, and now the neighborhood is becoming much more upscale and populated with strollers. With each transition, Christ Church has become something new and different, yet with a core group of long-timers that have maintained the church's vitality.

Two years into Rev. Cara Spacarelli's tenure, things are going swimmingly, and everyone thinks that she is magic. Rev. Cara, in turn, attributes much of her success to the supportive nature of the community. She says that change is the church's greatest strength: they'll try anything, even if they don't like it initially, and they've always been this way (one memorable instance: a newcomer who was made senior warden after less than six months' attendance!) Parishioners are not afraid to take ownership in their church, and they are equally unafraid to call on people to exercise their gifts. Rev. Cara builds on this by always keeping members aware of the big picture/long-term goals, and at the same time doing some things counter-intuitively: she won't do long-term programming ("it's harder for new people to join old groups than it is for everybody to join new groups"). She allows programming that addresses specific demographic groups and sees this as a long-term integration strategy (who wants to come to a group where you're the only young/middle-aged person there?)

Mother Cara sees her biggest success as, "bringing in the new, while keeping the old," or, as one parishioner said, "she has gotten things done without irritating the existing power structure." When asked what brings them hope about their church, people from Christ Church talk a lot about the "energy" they see in the parish: there are new faces—many of them young—and new events going on all the time. In the four days of my visit, I got to have burgers on the front lawn twice: once with kids and a water slide, and once with a brass band. The core group still wonders what the next major change will be in the neighborhood ("we hope the young families are going to stick around now") and how they will rise to meet it. If history is any indicator, change is not a problem for Washington, D. C.'s oldest Episcopal Church.

Photo: Kristin Carroccino. The National Cathedral, Washington, D.C., June 2012.

Community Beyond Our Walls. *Cara Spacarelli*

Cara is the rector of Christ Church on Capitol Hill in Washington, D.C. She wrote this post in response to our question "How does your parish practice evangelism?"

We think about what we as a community have to offer those beyond our walls that connects our gifts and the community's needs.

Tonight we have our first Grill & Chill of the summer: we grill out on our front lawn and put up a bunch of water-play, inflatable toys for the kids. Our neighborhood is high density and few people have yards, and even fewer people have grass on those yards. Grill & Chills offer those inside our wall a chance to gather, have a good time, and offer hospitality to the neighborhood. It offers the neighborhood a chance to hang out on a lawn and their kids to run through sprinklers—an experience they don't have too often.

Our neighborhood has as many dogs as kids, and every park has an accompanying dog park. So once a year on a Sunday, we celebrate St. Francis and invite everyone with their animals into the sanctuary for a Sunday morning Eucharist. Trust me, it works. One-fourth of the sanctuary is visitors, and they come up and ask me to bless their ailing pets; through tears in their eyes, they ask me to say a prayer for a loved animal that has passed away; they laugh at the giant German Shepherd who lays down in the middle of the aisle.

Our neighborhood has a very strong Sunday morning brunch culture and a Sunday outdoor market that is a tourist destination. No doubt there are more gathered in the market and the restaurants than all of the churches of the neighborhood combined. Every Palm Sunday, we move our worship to the street and process following a cross, playing trumpets, the children waving streamers and handing out palms from the market to the church. On the other liturgical end, we stand at the metro stop on Ash Wednesday and distribute ashes. Dozens of people stopped to receive the ashes, from Episcopal tourists from Atlanta who had missed attending services at the National Cathedral, to Catholics who had to decide whether it was better to receive ashes from an Episcopal priest than not receive at all, our own congregants on their way home from work, and strangers who silently walked up, lifted up their bangs, and bowed their heads.

Our faith offers something real to people. These simple events are ways for the church to connect to those outside our walls, but they shape our own faith, reminding us that our faith, our community offers something of substance to people. God asked us to go out into the world and make disciples of all nations, because our faith responds to a need that they have. Going outside our walls reminds us of that, and when a guest comes inside our walls, we listen to them— to the need that they have come to church looking to fill, and we let our church and our God respond.

Photo credit: Kristin Carroccino. Capitol Hill row houses. June 2012.

A Sense of Place: Cranston, Rhode Island, and St. David's on-the-Hill.
Kristin

We have affirmed in the last few days that we greatly prefer traveling on the back roads and by-ways compared to the theoretical efficiency of the Interstate highway system. It only took a few minutes of idling in standstill traffic on the beltways around Washington D.C., and Baltimore before we baffled our GPS and chose routes that were more interesting. When we left I-95, the countryside and city centers opened to us like jewel boxes, from grazing cows and local crab cake eateries in suburban Maryland to tightly packed row houses and fast streetcars that squeezed past us on Baltimore's narrow streets. We glimpsed New York City's hazy skyline from the George Washington Bridge in New Jersey. The interstate seemed inescapable in southern Connecticut, and the drive to Cranston, Rhode Island, took hours longer than expected. It made me wonder why thousands of people idle in cars on these routes every day. Do they know what lies beyond the barrage of Home Depots, Targets, McDonalds, and Motel 6s?

Eventually, when we had inched past Waterbury, New Haven, and New London, the traffic melted away along with billboards and construction sites, and we drove through a landscape that made us aware we had finally reached New England. Conifers in the forests lining the highway were much shorter than the lofty pines of the South; granite walls replaced limestone; the nearness of the ocean carried cool breezes to us. We had reached the "Ocean State" of Rhode Island and the site of our next parish visit.

The city of Cranston and the parish of St. David's on-the-Hill seem to be places in search of a core identity. The borders of east Cranston blend in with Providence, with its dueling grittiness and grandeur. In west Cranston, new subdivisions and retail developments are sprouting up and spreading out across agricultural areas that historically supported large dairy farms. More recently, small, organic fruit and vegetable farms promoting shares in Community Supported Agriculture are becoming more common. This city of 80,000 is arranged mostly by ethnic neighborhoods and has several lovely parks and an historic waterfront area. The city's website declares, "We're on the Move!" and educates readers that the Latin phrase on the city seal has been translated as "While I watch I care." Another nickname painted on signs around Cranston is "The Garden City." All of these attributes capture the vibe of this place, a mixture of pride in commercial growth, a nod to tight family bonds in its neighborhoods, and an appreciation for and cultivation of natural beauty.

During our visit at St. David's, we are enjoying the lovely gardens, bounteous offerings of food (their coffee hour today boasted a pot of authentic baked beans and a local style of calzone, pastries, spinach rolls, and more—wow!), and hospitality of a community asking some challenging questions about what it means to be St. David's. Faced with a decline

Photo: Kristin Carroccino: St. David's-on-the-Hill, Cranston, Rhode Island, June 2012.

in membership and resources over the past few decades, a number of small parishes in the Diocese of Rhode Island have been merging, hoping to become more efficient and at the same time more energized. St. David's has been in ongoing discernment about whether to merge with another local Episcopal church. There is some anxiety about this prospect, but also a sense of openness and curiosity about what the future holds.

This Sunday's Gospel reading was Jesus' parable about the mustard seed. In that story, we are reminded that a little bit of faith goes a long way. Sometimes our faith feels so small, like the tiny mustard seed, and we fear it is gone. As St. David's on-the-Hill continues to ask hard questions of themselves and engage the possibility of changing identities by merging with another church, they will be exercising a lot of faith. I look forward to hearing new stories of what the parish discovers as they detour from the familiar path they have known into rich unknown territory.

"We're the Church Willing to Ask Hard Questions." *Michael*

St. David's on-the-Hill is a wonderful community tucked away in a neighborhood on the west side of the city of Cranston, Rhode Island. They provided us a warm welcome and were extremely interested in our project and what we had to say. When I sat down with individuals and began to talk, nearly all of them told me the same two stories about their church. The first had to do with a proposed merger with a church across town (more on this below), and the second was about a man named Ray who made a strong impression on everyone he met.

Ray was an anchor to the parish for decades: he always wore a bow tie at church, he had a fantastic deep voice (useful as the voice of God during the yearly Sunday School skit) and he could whistle beautifully. For many decades of his life, Ray would unfailingly show up at church every Sunday and sit with the children to tell them Bible stories. He had a three-year rotation and he followed it through nearly three generations of children at St. David's before he died recently. As a mark of respect, the whole parish showed up in bow ties the next Sunday.

Everyone's story of Ray exemplifies what is strongest in the parish life of St. David's. Most of the interviewees had long-standing ties to the church, and their level of commitment is extremely high. Even as they face a merger, it seems that the dominant mentality among the congregation is, "just tell us what's going to happen, so we know where to show up." Members help one another through hard times and celebrate together with parish feasts and events in each season. They describe the church as their family and show a level of dogged devotion that exemplifies such a relationship. They even celebrate their children like a family: just as Ray devotedly told the young children their stories, the youth ministry thrives in dealing with the complex and heartfelt questioning of teenagers struggling to discover and create their own identities.

To worship with St. David's is to worship with a group who are very comfortable in their space and among one another, a group who know their roles and have played them well for many years. This church knows deep down—and with more than a little anxiety—something new is over the horizon. They have seen the changes in the larger church, in the neighborhood, in the culture that surrounds them, and they don't quite know what to make of it all. The parish's previous rector made the situation very clear when she explained to them in no uncertain terms that their financial situation was not sustainable for the long term, and among the options available to them, they chose to explore the possibility of merging with another congregation.

Now they are discussing in earnest with a church across town the various details, challenges, and possibilities that come along with such a proposition. The other church is ten miles away in a much more urban location, with a strong core of outreach ministries to persons experiencing homelessness on the streets of the downtown area they serve, and it seems the biggest area of contention—from what I could discern—is the decision about the buildings.

It was tempting to try to jump into the fray here, to offer suggestions and solutions; to problem-solve as the (so-called) objective stranger. However, as I observed the discussions and listened to the stories I became gradually more aware that the community of St. David's is a microcosm for the reality of the entire Episcopal Church. In the midst of a raft of difficult decisions, it seems that the biggest challenge is to put a definitive answer to the deeper questions of identity and purpose. The people of St. David's love their church with an unswerving devotion, but as I asked each of them about the church's interaction with the larger community, they spoke mostly of their collective participation in the ministries of other churches and various community groups. Asked what makes St. David's unique, answers often included "the people," the "acceptance," and "care for each other." "We have a lot of in-reach," said one man, "and maybe that's what attracts me to the church, to be honest."

All of this mirrors what I've heard again and again in other churches, and it seems to define the kind of honest bewilderment in the Episcopal Church on a larger scale: we're nice people, and we don't understand why more folks aren't showing up to take part! I feel hopeful for St. David's on-the-Hill: they have strong leadership, both lay and ordained, they have a large core of devoted and capable people, and there are plenty of youth attending. They routinely work together to help people in need, like the family of refugees for whom parishioners recently helped to find jobs and housing. Though they repeatedly mention their location as a problem (no bus lines serve the immediate area, and it's not on any main auto routes—many people don't know they exist), they actually have a pretty great building in an area of the city that's experiencing growth, something many parishes would envy. I think St. David's has a good chance of discerning a deeper identity (yes, they are a family, but a family that does what?) and rallying around something that brings life to both their members and their city.

Like the larger church, St. David's on-the-Hill has a deep latent identity and a rich trove of strength and capability. The only missing link—from my point of view—is the ability to talk about it well, to put a sharp point on just what it is that brings us all to church every week and how that can dovetail with the needs we see in our communities. That is to say: we need to put on our bow ties and start telling one another (and the world around us) the great stories of our faith.

Photo from www.stdavidsonthehill.net. These are windows inside St. David's on-the-Hill.

Tossing Out the Scripts. *Peter Lane*

Fr. Peter Lane is the interim priest at St. David's on-the-Hill in Cranston, Rhode Island. He writes in response to our question "What does it take to become an evangelizing church community?"

My first notable experience with evangelism didn't go so well. I was about 16 and our youth group got roped into an afternoon of evangelizing on Nauset Beach on Cape Cod. It was the middle of July, we'd been trained for our work, given a basic outline of a script to use for each encounter, and dressed in khakis, white shirts and ties…in the middle of July…on the beach…we set off to save souls. I hated every minute of it, and I'm pretty sure not a single soul was saved.

I've changed my approach to evangelism these days. I've tossed out the scripts and I tend not to wander the beach looking for souls to save. But it's funny—the uniform is still important. Living in Rhode Island where the Roman Catholic Church still holds significant sway in the wider culture, I find that wearing a collar opens up all sorts of opportunities for me to talk with people about the tender spots in their lives. I'm regularly stopped in the grocery store, or picking up dry cleaning, even filling up at the gas station, and asked if I have a minute to talk or say a prayer. I've come to welcome these encounters as true opportunities for evangelism—to share what I have learned about the amazing love of God, and how many times it has pulled me out of some pretty deep holes. And in the end, that's all any of us want to know for sure—that there's hope for us, that God is present and active and still working out salvation for each of us.

As we think about ways that we can become an evangelizing church community, a couple of things stand out for me. The first is for each of us to remember those moments in our own lives when God's amazing grace lifted us up out of whatever dark or hopeless place we'd stumbled into—evidence from our own stories of Good News, of God's saving hand. This is the bread we have to share with a hungry world.

And that leads to the second thing for us to think about and embrace—there are a lot of hungry people in this world. Physical hungers to be sure, but emotional and spiritual hungers too, even and maybe particularly among those who appear to be physically well fed. The world around us is starving for Good News, for a sense of hope, for something to believe in once again. All we are called to do as a witnessing community of faith is share with those who are hungry how we have been fed and sustained, and then invite them to the feast.

So, in the end, it seems to be a rather simple matter of remembering those stories of grace in our own lives, being sensitive to the hungers of those around us, and being willing to invite them to the place that feeds and gives us strength for the journey. No ties, collars, or scripts, required.

We Teach Evangelism. *Sara Clarke*

As I started to think about the word evangelical, and what it really means to me, I looked up the definition, and Miriam Webster defines it as this: of, relating to, or being in agreement with the Christian gospel especially as it is presented in the four Gospels.

However, when I really think about The Word, and the negative feelings it stirs up and how it relates to our current society, I automatically think about Billy Graham, fanatical ideas, and in-your-face-unrelenting religion.

It is easy to understand why we as Episcopalians are afraid to use the word "evangelical." The word itself conjures up images that make us uncomfortable—because as Episcopalians, we don't like to be told how to feel, or (audible gasp) what to think. You can guide us in a particular direction, point us gently to the answer, but please, whatever you do, don't tell us what to do, feel, or think.

But does that mean we aren't evangelical? Certainly, "we are in agreement with the Christian gospel especially as it presented in the four Gospels?" Aren't we?

As a child, being Episcopalian in a state that is predominately Roman Catholic, I never much talked about religion, my faith, or my beliefs in my everyday life. I was different from most of my school friends. And while I felt very lucky to not have to go to that foreign-sounding CCD [Confraternity of Christian Doctrine] class, there was part of me that felt left out, and misunderstood. I spent four years at a Catholic middle school, which only underscored what I had always believed; that I was one lucky girl to be an Episcopalian, and thank goodness we never had to go to confession.

Growing up as a parishioner at St. David's on-the-Hill in Cranston, Rhode Island, my parents showed me that being involved in church life was never an option, it was a way of life. Still, we never spoke about it on any sort of cerebral level. It was much more innate than that. We were always involved in church activities, be it social or prayerful, fun or fellowship. Church was what we did and the community that we embraced.

But in my years as a camper, counselor, and now fundraiser at the Episcopal Conference Center (ECC) in Pascoag, RI, we talked about God. We talked about the Gospel. . . all the time! We were encouraged to talk about our beliefs and how they related to the outside world, and we never apologized for being an Episcopal camp. Of course, sticking with the Episcopalian theme, we never told anyone how to feel or how to think!

What we did instead of telling people what do, feel or think, is teach. We taught people how to be kind and accepting, how to work hard and how to play hard. And maybe most importantly, we were taught to spread the word of God. Hang onto your hats, boys and girls, I do believe we were taught to be evangelical.

Before you get all nervous thinking that the Ocean State has converted all Episcopalians into fanatical in-your-face religious freaks, let me be clear: Not once do I remember the word "evangelical" being used. Not once! I was being taught the Gospel, how it related to my life, and how I could teach it to others. I was being taught how to be evangelical in the true sense of the word. What a wonderful gift!

To start each camp week at ECC, we would begin each staff meeting with this prayer:

> *Almighty God, you have so linked our lives with one another, that all we do or say effects, for good or ill, all other lives. Deliver us from the service of self alone, that we may do the work you have given us to do, in truth and beauty, and for the common good. For the sake of him who came among us as one who serves, through Jesus Christ our Lord, Amen.*

As the Episcopal Church continues to spread the Good News, and to teach the Gospel in a productive, purposeful way, I challenge each and every one of us to be evangelical: Don't shy away from religious discussions. Be proud to be Episcopalian. Engage others in discussion. We must continue. . . to "do the work God has given us to do," in truth and beauty and for the common good."

Amen!

Sara Clarke is a graduate of the University of Rhode Island. She is currently the Events Manager at Providence Children's Museum, owner of Emma's Edibles, a funky innovative chocolate experience, and she works in the Development Office of the Episcopal Conference Center. A career Sunday School teacher, Sara is also a member of the vestry at St. David's on-the-Hill Episcopal Church in Cranston, Rhode Island.

Snapshots of Evangelism. *Michael*

As we approached the six-week mark of our journey: Kristin and I reflected and compiled some snapshots of the ways we had seen individuals and churches living out evangelism:

† Dinners, bake sales, plant sales, craft sales, etc.—things that put the parish on the map and invite everyone in the area to come and see what's going on.

† Partnering with nonprofits to host medical clinics or other services for those in need.

† Allowing local school choirs to utilize the worship space for music concerts.

† Inviting in Girl Scouts, Boy Scouts, AA, and other community groups to use the space.

† Having bracelets made as part of a formation program that people still proudly wear months later.

† Putting out water toys for neighborhood children on the front lawn, hosting concerts outside.

† Starting a church on the street during the Occupy Wall Street movement.

† Providing Ashes to Go during Ash Wednesday.

† Advent graffiti on a prominent downtown church's retaining wall.

† Passing out beans and rice to the needy in the community.

† Cold-calling people from the phone book to discover community needs and desires.

† Clergy wearing collars in public and being willing to engage people in spiritual conversations in public places.

† Ringing the church bell on a regular schedule as a community clock.

† Baptisms at the beach.

† Inviting people to church.

† Looking around to see the people on the margins and inviting them in for worship.

† Free Vacation Bible School and low-cost preschool programs for the whole neighborhood.

† Installing solar panels as an example of good environmental stewardship.

† Handmade pottery crosses for every visitor—from artists in the congregation.

† Offering guided tours of historical church structures.

† People lounging in a shady green downtown cemetery during their lunch break.

† Welcoming in refugee families and helping them get settled.

† Mass on the Grass: pets invited!

† Monthly children's service where the kids gather around the altar.

† Community transport services for the homebound and elderly.

† Community gardens and labyrinths.

† Beautiful worship spaces open to the public.

† Visible and integral roles for children in the service.

† Wicker chairs with cushions for people made uncomfortable by plain wooden pews.

† Hosting community e-waste recycling.

† Palm Sunday processions along the city streets.

† Outdoor Stations of the Cross.

† Making friends outside our faith tradition—celebrating the commonalities.

† Praying with strangers in need.

† Weekly alms ministry.

† Thrift stores and bookshops.

Image: Icon of St. Columba. Public domain.

Time off in the Mountains. *Michael*

This week, we finally made our way out of the heavy traffic that is New England and into the heavy forest that is the White Mountains of New Hampshire for a week of rest and family time. It has been nice to take some time away from *Boats without Oars* writing and interviewing to just let it all settle. We have had nothing but rain since we got to our hotel, so we've been enjoying the mountains simply by driving into and out of the clouds and repeatedly telling the kids things like "there's a beautiful waterfall over there when the weather's clear!" Ah well; Kristin and I lived in New Hampshire in 2002, so at least we already know what it looks like. Still, even though this is a "vacation" week for us, we are curiously eyeing the local Episcopal churches in the towns along our driving tour.

Today it was in North Conway, New Hampshire. Christ Church Episcopal was right on the intersection of two major roads, and only minutes from the crowded Main Street shops. It had beautiful woodwork, a white picket

Photo: *Kristin Carroccino. Cannon Mountain Aerial Tramway, New Hampshire. June 2012.*

fence, and a thrift shop on the grounds. It looks like a lively place, at least on a drive-by in the rain. I find myself wondering how the dynamics of various churches work. How does a tourist town, industrial town, or capital city affect the workings and character of a church? How does a church serve a community whose members are out every day—especially weekends—during the tourist season operating aerial tramways, driving buses for moose-viewing tours, or cleaning hotel rooms?

These are the types of questions that continue to fuel our wonderful, long road trip. We have reached our northernmost destination this week and are ready to turn west. Amazingly, the questions we ponder and answers we devise about the Episcopal Church along the miles continue to strengthen our desire to visit more churches and hear their stories.

Photo: Kristin and Michael Carroccino, New Hampshire, June 2012.

Journal Entry: June 26, Lincoln, New Hampshire.
Kristin

I've noticed yesterday, and this morning, how utterly and quickly frustrated I become when surrounded by chaos, and most especially when I can't find something I need in the clutter—or even when I have misplaced something. Anxiety rises in me. This morning, I couldn't find my blue jeans, which were, in fact, in the clothing drawer all along. When, on first glance, I didn't notice them, my head felt hot and stuffy; all my muscles tightened. I looked in the closet, dug through dirty clothes, felt angry, worried that I'd lost my one pair of jeans. Then, I looked again in the drawer and found them. I spent so much emotional energy on something that wasn't actually lost! At its core, this must be a panic of losing control, of needing to know where everything is to feel safe. It's easy to feel out of control all these miles from home and forget how untidy the world really is, in all its maddening and glorious chaos. Knowing where everything is all of the time doesn't guarantee a safer or better existence, but, for now, I'm really glad I found my jeans.

Evangelism. *Terry Pierce*

A Tuesday evening in early spring in Pennsylvania: I drive into the parking lot of a small stone church with large red doors. There are four or five cars in the parking lot, much as I would expect on a night when there is a meeting of a recovery group. I cautiously enter the side doors. I follow the sound of voices down a hallway. Too late, I realize that the conversation is not what I would hear at a recovery meeting. As I am turning to retrace my steps, a woman's voice bounds out of the room. "May I help you?" she says. I respond that I'm looking for the AA meeting. She replies, "That's Thursday night. We're having a Bible study. Would you like to join us?" From a great distance, I hear a voice that must be my own say "Sure" and I find myself stepping into the room.

Image: public domain.

The woman introduces herself as the rector, though I don't know what that means. I notice the peculiar collar she wears, but I don't know what that means either. My time in churches has mostly been in church basements at AA meetings and my exposure to priests and pastors has been nil. I don't recall what they were studying but the conversation was interesting. The rector invited me to attend church on Sunday and told me a teaser about what she was going to preach. I made no commitment.

As surely as I don't know what drew me to that church on the wrong night for an AA meeting or whose voice it was that agreed to enter their Bible study room, I don't know what force drew me from my bed on a chilled early spring morning to go to church. It was an activity I had not participated in since my youth. I was uncomfortable and I went. Some of the "Bible study people" greeted me and invited me to sit with them. I don't remember very much about that day: The books were confusing and the standing, sitting and kneeling was incomprehensible. On Tuesday night, I visited the Bible study again. The following Sunday, I found myself once again venturing from bed into the chill morning and joining the "Bible study people" in church.

I was a stranger with little in common with the members of that small Bible study. I was a liberal feminist, Al Gore bumper sticker, recovering alcoholic, single, working person in the midst of a group of conservative, retired, Bush bumper sticker couples who had the traditional Episcopalian enjoyment of a good bottle of wine. They invited me into their house and made me welcome there. Eighteen months later, they stood up with me as I was confirmed in the Episcopal Church.

Terry Pierce is the Pastoral Leader of St. James Episcopal Church in Taylor, Texas.

Interview: Brother Curtis Almquist.
Kristin and Michael

This past weekend, we traveled to Emery House near West Newbury, Massachusetts, the retreat house for the Society of St. John the Evangelist. Over a plate of cookies and later a stroll through the grounds of this peaceful place where our children picked strawberries and watched a Brother tending to the community chickens, we spent time talking with Brother Curtis Almquist about his reflections on evangelism and the religious life. He is a person who is very comfortable in his own skin and capable of listening and reflecting on a very deep level: he pondered each of our questions at length and answered them thoroughly and thoughtfully. As he talked, we recognized a few themes emerging that—even as Brother Curtis literally lives a cloistered life—resonated with the kinds of discussions we've been having across the country with people about how they experience God in the church.

Evangelism, Curtis says, is simply helping people to hear the Good News of Jesus. Pressed on what this Good News might be, he veritably lights up when explaining for the first of many times during our visit that "God loves, God uses, God calls, God knows each and every one of us fully as the person we are—not the one we wish we were, not who others would like us to be." No one knows each of us more fully than God does, and, even so, no one loves us more completely. People hear Good News from the inside out, and evangelism comes forth naturally from hearing this message and wholly knowing it from "the tops of our heads to the bottom of our toes." When we really know the Good News, we can't contain it; "it bursts forth from us as involuntarily as the fragrance from flowers."

People come to monasteries seeking something different, unique even for each individual, something that can reconnect them at a fundamental level to their deep, and deeply loved, selves. Brother Curtis explains that the Society of Saint John the Evangelist does a lot of work with spiritual formation, with helping people develop a vocabulary to hear the Good News from the inside out. He says that their primary task is to help people learn to "pray their lives." They seek to reconnect the spiritual with the rest of life: "Jesus didn't say: 'I came that you might have abundant *spiritual* life!'" People go to church, he says, to receive that same kind of reconnection, to have something to pray with their lives—so that their lives aren't just a bunch of compartments. Until we know such connection fully, we will not trust that we have the kind of insight or authority we need to share that Good News with authenticity.

People in our world have lost their bearings: so many changes are happening in the culture and in the church, and the things that we all learned to take for granted in childhood, the things we saw as points of anchorage, are no longer there for us. In Brother Curtis' experience, people come to the monastery as a place of refuge—a place that will welcome the outsider—because they are adrift; they are *lost*. The religious life has always been eccentric (at the edge) rather than concentric (at the center), a place of liminality, so when people come seeking direction from the Brothers, they feel safe in asking, "how now should I live?" or "how can I go about being a follower of Jesus?" Curtis says that people today find themselves reluctant to commit to anything, and that affects every facet of our society, including marriage and church. Instead of a place to plug in, the people he often meets at the retreat house are simply looking for *sanctuary*.

As our interview began to wind down, Curtis told us,

> I can speak about evangelism as a monk: when I speak to people, I am there at their initiation, at their invitation. The most important news that people can hear from Jesus is that Jesus loves them in the context of knowing them. Most people have considerable resistance around that. Everyone's got their own story about why it is they don't deserve love. Our ministry is about uncovering, or recovering, or discovering with another person where and how they can know that God adores them.

Brother Curtis' words linger in the air, and we wish we could stay longer. However, our children, who have been mostly quiet in the room during our conversation, have reached a level of restlessness that makes a walk outdoors an alluring prospect. Along the way, we discover baby chicks and goslings, a strawberry patch, and fields of hay as we walk to the Merrimack River through verdant summer fields.

While we pack up our things and prepare to leave, we are humbled by our time spent with Brother Curtis and more deeply inquisitive. Brother Curtis speaks only from his perspective as one called to live the religious life as a monastic Episcopalian, a church tradition that he believes contains a lot of Good News. He gives thanks to God that the church is a very diverse body, and that evangelism covers a broad spectrum.

Some questions we are left pondering: should this be any different for the rest of us? How do those eccentrics of the religious life inform our understanding of evangelism as people at the center (traditional churches)? How do people transform from seeking sanctuary to being sanctuary for others?

Brother Curtis Almquist is a member of the Society of St. John the Evangelist, and formerly a parish priest. He is active as a spiritual director and retreat leader, and lives at SSJE's rural monastery, Emery House, in West Newbury, Massachusetts. For more information about the brothers' life and ministry visit www.SSJE.org.

Photo: Kristin Carroccino. A walk with Brother Curtis Almquist, Society of St. John the Evangelist Monastery, Emery House, West Newbury, Massachusetts. June 2012.

Evangelism = Companions on the Journey.
Jodi Baron

Evangelism. What does that word even mean anymore? Evangelism has been hijacked, distorted, and convoluted in so many contradictory ways, it seems to me, that it's almost impossible to land on a common operating definition to have a conversation around. For the sake of this musing, I will attempt to draw out my own working definition of evangelism.

I do what I do, I am who I am, because of the love I have for God. That love I've grown to know and embody has been revealed to me through the life, death, and resurrection of Jesus. To have this love, this incarnation of the essence of God, is too wonderful for me to not want to share with others this love inside of me. As I learn to love myself more, because of my identity being that of a child of God, I am learning how to look at others with that love.

The hospital is the perfect example for me as to what evangelism is meaning to me right now. Every day, I go to the hospital and pretend to be a Chaplain for patients who find themselves amidst one of the scariest times of their life. Maybe they just got a new diagnosis, maybe they are facing surgery, maybe they are failing to thrive, maybe they just had a baby...every room is different and each person holds their own sense of who God is and where God is during this time of their life. My job is to enter into their story and invite them to explore what gives them strength. I invite them to think about what role God plays in their life: through sickness and health. And as I do that, I sense that I am being the hands and feet of God. I sense that I am presenting the caring listening of our God to people in desperate need of a God who cares about them right now, in this mortal experience.

But not everyone has this opportunity to pretend to be chaplains. So what I'm reflecting on now is how can I empower the true ministers of the church that THEY can be that presence to folks they have connection with, how can the ministry I equip them with on Sunday impact them to go and be (in the words of theologian Samuel Wells) *WITH* people regardless of the theology their head tells them to believe?

I am convinced that being in community is where this happens. In a healthy community, we have opportunity for equipping leaders to be with people, not fix people. The healing that so many people, it seems, are looking for is the healing that can only come from being heard, seen, listened to, cared about. They want to know that God, indeed, loves them unconditionally, right? Isn't that what we all want? To be known? To be loved? To be accepted just as we are?

My challenge this summer is to learn how to [bracket] my judgments and assumptions about people based on socially constructed stereotypes, and allow the child of God (that GOD loved enough to become human to save) to emerge and be loved.

Jodi Baron is now a priest serving Grace Episcopal Church in Holland, Michigan. She and her husband have been married for 14 years and have three children.

Church Beyond the Walls. *Edmund Harris*

Several weeks ago, my partner Michael and I had the privilege of hosting Michael and Kristin and their children Caedmon and Mirella in our home for supper. Along with several other folks from the Diocese of Rhode Island where I serve, we had an intriguing conversation about where we see new life in the Episcopal Church in the 21st Century. During our time together, I also had the opportunity to share with them about two new church initiatives here in Rhode Island in which I've taken part.

The first initiative is a new worship and evangelism ministry that emerged from the Occupy Wall St. Movement. For four months last autumn and early winter, a group of Episcopalians from congregations in the diocese met weekly on Sunday afternoons for worship and hospitality in Burnside Park in downtown Providence, the site of Occupy Providence. We called ourselves "Church at Occupy Providence," and quickly became a ministry shared by laity and clergy from around the diocese and beyond. Together with Occupy Providence protesters, homeless persons, and other guests, we gathered in the park week after week to proclaim the Gospel, share in Christ's Body and Blood, and experience Christ's presence in one another. On Ash Wednesday, emboldened by these experiences of taking church outside of the walls of our building, some of the people who had been present in the park offered "Ashes to Go" in various depots and commuter stations around the state. As in the park, we encountered deep spiritual as well as physical hunger in the people we met.

Seeking to build on these experiences, Church of the Epiphany in East Providence, where I'm Assistant to the Rector, has been awarded a grant from the Congregational Development Commission of the diocese to initiate a pilot ministry called Church Beyond the Walls. The overarching need that Church Beyond the Walls will seek to address is hunger: physical as well as spiritual hunger. Although the people who worshiped at Church at Occupy Providence came from diverse backgrounds, what we shared in common was *hunger*. Some people in the park were physically hungry, including homeless people. Other people expressed deep spiritual hunger. Many said they desired a relationship with God, but did not feel comfortable stepping inside a church. Some, especially those who served or worshiped in "housed" congregations, expressed hunger for a church that was willing to come outside its buildings in order to focus on God's mission. As in the Eucharist, where physical and spiritual hunger converged in the park, we found ourselves walking on holy ground.

The community we envision at Church Beyond the Walls will continue to be an intentionally mixed community of homeless and housed people, young and old, and will gather on a weekly basis for a celebration of the Eucharist. Worship will be followed by hospitality, including a meal for all. CBW will partner with the George Hunt Help Center, a drop-in center in downtown Providence with the mission of offering hospitality to homeless women and men. We also hope that Church Beyond the Walls will initiate a coordinated effort to bring church outside of buildings in other ways throughout the diocese on a regular basis.

The second initiative is a new Episcopal Service Corps community that we hope to plant in the diocese in 2013 called Jonathan Daniels House. Beginning in 2010, a diocesan task force in which I took part sought to consider how the Episcopal Church could maintain an active presence in South Providence and the surrounding communities following the closure of the last Episcopal congregation there in 2009. How, we asked, can vital ministry of the Episcopal Church in the South Providence area emerge from the needs and hopes of the communities there? What unique attributes can the Episcopal Church bring to such communities? And with what organizations or programs can the Episcopal Church partner in the South Providence area in order to build the Kingdom of God in our city? As we engaged in our work as a task force, the possibilities for ministry in the South Providence area crystallized around the idea of planting an Episcopal Service Corps community. The Episcopal Service Corps is an expanding constellation of over 20 young-adult, residential service programs across the Episcopal Church. Participants in Episcopal Service Corps programs live together, work alongside service agencies embedded in local communities, and engage in vocational and spiritual discernment for a period of 9 to 11 months. They are provided with housing, a stipend to cover living expenses, and health insurance.

Early on, there was consensus around naming Episcopal Service Corps community in Providence in honor of Jonathan Daniels. Daniels was a seminarian in the Episcopal Church who answered the call of Martin Luther King, Jr., in 1965 for students and clergy to join the struggle for civil rights. Although many people recognize Daniels as a martyr of the Civil Rights Movement, fewer people know that he spent time ministering in South Providence before traveling to the South. We could think of no better way to honor Daniels than by founding a new community whose mission will seek to continue his witness in the places where he served.

Living and working alongside residents of South Providence communities, Jonathan Daniels House interns will seek to build the Kingdom of God by struggling for justice, striving for reconciliation among all people, and maintaining the presence of the church in the city. A fivefold structure will enable Jonathan Daniels House interns to do this: They will work in local agencies committed to justice and reconciliation, live simply and sustainably in Christian community, commit to a life of communal and personal prayer, participate in regular theological and critical reflection on their work, and engage in discernment about God's call in their lives. Jonathan Daniels House will have a wide-reaching impact in South Providence and the surrounding neighborhoods, forming diverse new communities of people, and expanding the reach of existing organizations and programs. We also hope that Jonathan Daniels House will also have a significant impact on the life of the diocese, nourishing a regular young-adult presence, encouraging collaboration among parishes, missions, and diocesan organizations to become involved, and connecting the diocese to the wider church in service.

In many ways, this is a tender time in the life of the Episcopal Church, a time when most dioceses and many congregations are coming to terms with decline. This is certainly true Rhode Island. Here, many of our congregations are not sustainable in the long term. Earlier this year, our cathedral closed. Certainly, one way to greet these realities is with anxiety and fear. Many do. And to be fair, I can see how for some, it's frightening when fewer bodies are in the pews and the infrastructure we've come to know as "church" is crumbling. At the same time, I believe that the Holy Spirit is moving in and through the challenges the Episcopal Church faces to call us to become something new: a new community of disciples concerned less with church maintenance and more with cooperating with God's mission. From my perspective, this is already happening right under our noses here in Rhode Island. Even as we are facing into real decline, the ground has never been more fertile for new forms of church to emerge in our midst. Indeed, as the collect from the Easter Vigil promises, "things which were cast down are being raised up, and things which had grown old are being made new." (*Book of Common Prayer*, 285)

Edmund Harris recently relocated to the Diocese of Olympia where he lives with his husband Michael. He formerly served as Priest and Organizer of Church Beyond the Walls, a street church community rooted in the Episcopal tradition in Providence, Rhode Island.

Episcopalians in Critical Care?
We've Been There Before.
Meredith Henne Baker

In a recent article for the *New York Times*, Ross Douthat[18] took the pulse of the Episcopalian Church and delivered some grave news: Should they continue on their "liberal" path, "their fate is nearly certain: they will change, and change, and die." So, is the Church on her deathbed? Episcopalians have heard that before; two hundred years ago, to be precise, and in the cradle of American Episcopalianism: the Commonwealth of Virginia.

American defeat of the English in the Revolutionary War meant an end to Anglican dominance in Virginia. In the new republic, the Church of England, Virginia's official state church throughout the colonial years, no longer enjoyed a

Photo of William Meade from www.anglicanhistory.org.

privileged status. Throughout the 1780s, its glebe lands were sold off, the number of Episcopal ministers declined statewide from over ninety to twenty-eight, and it lost all state support. Winds blew through the broken walls of abandoned rural churches and birds drank from unused baptismal fonts. The church changed its name to the Protestant Episcopal Church, but no new moniker could save it.

After his ordination in 1811, Episcopal priest William Meade heard tales circulated "that there was something unsound in mind or eccentric in character, at any rate a want of good common sense" about him to have made the mistake of joining a church with such "fallen and desperate fortunes." As his first

---

[18]http://www.nytimes.com/2012/07/15/opinion/sunday/douthat-can-liberal-christianity-be-saved.html?_r=1&hp&utm_source=buffer&buffer_share=0bdb9

post, he took over a pulpit in Alexandria, Virginia, that had been vacated by a bigamist.

Besides (sound familiar?) a precipitous loss of finances, a withering supply of suitable ministers, and an inability to compete with the far more entertaining style of the Methodists and Baptists, there was that whole liberal thing. Even back in the early republic, Episcopalians were often considered unorthodox, embracing the ideas of freethinkers and French revolutionaries, preaching sermons that evangelicals considered merely "moral" rather than scriptural. In 1792, Episcopalian Elizabeth Carrington, Chief Justice John Marshall's sister-in-law, despaired of the "modern philosophers" that peppered her Richmond congregation—wealthy, educated, and spiritually barren. "But blessed be God, in spite of the enlightened, as they call themselves, and in spite of Godwin, Paine, and others, we still…endeavor to preserve the religion of our fathers," she wrote.

And what of that "religion of our fathers?" Douthat, quoting liberal Protestant scholar Gary Dorrien, remarks, "the Christianity that animated causes such as the Social Gospel and the civil rights movement was much more dogmatic than present-day liberal faith. Its leaders had a "deep grounding in Bible study, family devotions, personal prayer and worship." They argued for progressive reform in the context of "a personal transcendent God . . . the divinity of Christ, the need of personal redemption and the importance of Christian missions."

A renewed focus on aspects of "historic Christianity" that are worth saving and promoting seems to be what Douthat prescribes to salvage the denomination. Historical precedent would indicate that this is a pretty fair estimate. Emphasis on personal and corporate spiritual disciplines and missions is, in part, what brought Episcopalianism back from the brink two hundred years ago. Influential evangelical reformers in the late 18th and early 19th centuries, like Devereaux Jarrett, Richard Channing Moore, and William Meade, encouraged their congregants to host prayer meetings in their homes and have family devotions. (Their detractors called them "Methodists" for their trouble.) Episcopalian women assumed leadership positions and founded Sunday Schools and charities for the poor. Ministers also created missionary organizations that sent evangelists to the neglected western regions of the state and a seminary in Virginia to train up a new generation of priests.

Virginia's Episcopal churches began to grow in membership and the institution flourished remarkably for the next century. Like Peter's indefatigable mother-in-law, revived by Christ, the church went immediately from sickbed to service.

Scholars like Robert Putnam and Charles Murray note that adherence to religious institutions has been falling for decades; this isn't just the Episcopal Church's struggle.[19] Many (like myself, full disclosure) who attend Episcopal churches would not agree with Douthat that their priests aren't "offering anything you can't already get from a purely secular liberalism." On the congregational level in an Episcopal Church, you will likely find Bible studies, nursery schools, people who pray, and brown sacks full of sandwiches for the homeless in the foyer. If the institution's excesses of liberal theology, environmentalism, and syncretism are the ailment, the Episcopal Church has faced down other similarly daunting accusations in her past.

And history shows us she has changed, and changed, and lived.

Meredith Henne Baker is the author of The Richmond Theater Fire: Early America's First Great Disaster, *(March 2012, LSU Press) which explores in part the fire's role as a catalyst for reformation in the Episcopal Church. More at* www.theaterfirebook.com . *She attends historic Christ Church on Capitol Hill in Washington, D.C.*

---

[19]http://www.washingtonpost.com/blogs/guest-voices/post/can-christianity-be-revived/2012/07/18/gJQAD7jXtW_blog.html

Questions

How do we become "sanctuary" for others?

How does our community of faith engage the surrounding neighborhood?

What does "welcome" mean?

Beyond traditional parish and Diocesan funding, what other resources might your church develop as you engage the greater community?

What does being church "outside the walls" mean in your community?

JULY 2012: SAILING

What is Adventure? *Kristin*

This week marks the halfway point of our vast journey across the United States to gather, learn, and discern both what is going on inside the Episcopal church and within ourselves as individual members of that great body. It also marks the point on this adventure that we turn and head west. We have spent the last eight weeks immersing ourselves in southern and eastern Episcopal churches, observing worship styles both "high" and "low" in locales with long histories in Anglicanism. Now we will be visiting places that were on the edges of the American frontier in the nineteenth century. Europeans who settled the American West, seemed to be forever looking for new life, whether they were escaping from, or prospecting for, opportunity.

Early European-American settlers certainly had an itch, willing to risk their lives—or those of their friends and families on tall but small ships—crossing the vast and often violent Atlantic in pursuit of a romanticized "New World." For the average person, I imagine that had they been prospering in the motherland, they would not have placed their hopes and dreams on unseen territory. Whatever relational discomfort or lack these people had, from individuals down on their luck and willing to be indentured as servants or to the English, we now call "Puritans" who sought religious liberty from England, a deep desire for transformation and independence probably kept them hopeful on dark nights.

I watched the documentary 180° *South* recently. In it, the founder of the outdoor clothing company Patagonia, Yvon Chouinard, remarked, "The word adventure has gotten overused. For me, when everything goes wrong, that's when adventure starts." Chouinard was poking fun at the cultural idea many westerners seem to hold—that adventure is almost like an emotion—a thrill one gets from trying something new, or maybe even just daydreaming about it. I think he is correct. The forces in our lives that most powerfully shape us are those unexpected and maybe even unpleasant events—the wrong turn on the trail that yields a new vista and a new understanding of how better to read a map, the lack of ingredients in the pantry that forces new culinary creativity, the unrelenting unpredictability of how friends and family members are "supposed to" behave. If we had kept plodding along on the familiar path, new growth would have less likely occurred.

Both individuals and church communities seek adventure, but do we really know what we are pursuing? When we imagine new possibilities, adventure even, are we prepared for the journey and how transformational growth most likely won't happen without some wrong turns and illnesses along the way, and a good measure of heartache?

As I sit near our hotel room on this chilly first morning of July in the far northern Appalachian Mountains, I can form a prediction of what I think I will experience in the next few weeks, but if I linger too long in my reverie, I may miss some of the learning opportunities and growth that are there for the taking. I must lay aside many of my preconceptions and embrace the "adventure" that is to come. I look to the West and seek transformation. I am eager to look back at the end of this *Boats without Oars* journey and reflect on the changes I see within my own family and within the Episcopal Church, and look forward with hope to see new growth happening everywhere along the way.

The image of the eagle is often associated with St. John the Evangelist. Public Domain.

Is There Any Hope for Us? *Michael*

In each of my interviews, I have finished by asking people: "of all the things you see going on in your church right now, what gives you the most hope for the future?" After reflecting on the first two months of *Boats without Oars,* I find that it is a good question to ask myself as well. In July, midway through our journey, we stopped through Indianapolis to visit the Episcopal Church's General Convention, and I had the privilege of standing in a convention hall with thousands of people who all sang with one strong voice "Joyful, joyful, we adore you." What an experience—a crowning point in our travels to be sure—but as I read through the reports of the tension and difficulty happening at the convention, I was tempted to revert back to a more skeptical view of the church. But, it is the very messiness and discomfort of our church's character that I think exemplify what I am coming to appreciate more about Episcopalians as I pray and talk with them around the country.

Earlier this year, whenever I described our project, I always began by explaining that its genesis came from the ever-present anxiety about the future of our church. I am convinced, I explained, that the possibilities and the limitations of our future are already contained in the stories we tell today. What I have found in listening to the stories this summer is that the Episcopal Church occupies a very unique place in the religious landscape of America. We are a people who are doggedly committed to wrestling with our faith—and often with most other areas of our lives—in an atmosphere of open and generous inquiry. Because of this, we tolerate levels of ambiguity and uncertainty that would (and does) drive many away, and in so doing, we cultivate a deep sense of awe and mystery of the divine. Even so, we work out all of this tension within our communities, and the deep and abiding commitment of our church seems to be that we make room for, and listen to, every voice at the table. (I'm not saying we're always great at this. Rather, it is a part of our core makeup.)

One parishioner put it well: "we are condemned to inefficiency." He was essentially correct: the Episcopal Church is not a one-size-fits-all brand of faith. Asked about what best facilitates their connection with God in the church, many of my interviewees said something like, "I get to be who I am without being judged," or "nobody tells me what to think." And so it is this, I think, that brings about the kind of honest—and messy—struggle that defines the hierarchy and process of our church. There are about as many people in the Episcopal Church as in the city of Houston, Texas, and yet we require the largest governing body outside of India to make our decisions. This "inefficiency," though difficult to bear as a body, is an outgrowth of the strength of character within our denomination that seeks to honor the dignity of all people. It is, in many respects, the quality I see in my church that gives me the most hope for its future.

We live in a world that, by contrast, pushes the weak or discordant voices to the margins. If differences exist on a given issue, American culture ratchets them into full-blown polar opposites and then demands that we choose between one extreme and the other. In an all-or-nothing culture, many are pushed toward having either a rigidly defined faith or none at all, and increasingly they choose to leave the church. In my travels, I have met disaffected people from all places on the spectrum of American spirituality, and the hospitality they have found in Episcopal churches has given them a sanctuary, a protected space where they can begin to "work out their salvation in fear and trembling" within community (Phil. 2:12). We are a church staunchly committed to the center, the middle way, and we live in a culture where the middle is the margin. As such, we are well poised to address the needs of people on the outside who need a place to belong. Efficient? Not so much. Hopeful? Absolutely.

Journal Entry: July 7. South Haven, Michigan. *Kristin*

Something is being loosed in me here in South Haven—I feel my soul being tumbled about like the chunks of beer bottles that become prized Lake Michigan "beach glass." The lake is as vast as an ocean, extending for miles in my view as I sit here under a pergola strung with green vines in the backyard of yet another set of people who have welcomed us without questions, gifted us with their time and space. Robins, wrens, blue jays, finches, and lake waves, serenade me. There are so many Edens always waiting for us.

This morning, I sat for hours on the beach below, at the foot of steep stairs that lead up to our hosts' home. I floated in the waves, found perfect rocks, and precious hours in which I didn't care about the time of day. It was healing. I feel both whole and more broken apart. For thirty minutes, a ladybug explored the terrain of my hand, stopping occasionally to preen on a knuckle. It seemed to be flight-impaired, so I eventually liberated it in a cool, green hedge. I found a rock, perfect and slightly round, flat, bi-colored. I want to wear it close to my heart, to remember.

Yesterday, Father Michael Ryan said, "the beginning of hospitality is learning how to receive—basically giving up control." I'm learning over this summer how much control I need to release, how much more I need to learn to receive.

A Sense of Place: South Haven, Michigan, and Church of the Epiphany.
Kristin

"This place has worked some magic on me," responded a new friend from South Haven when I asked her about her experiences with Church of the Epiphany, here in this small town on the vast shores of Lake Michigan. My eyes smarted with tears as she spoke, because I quickly identified with that feeling. As we leave South Haven today and travel north and west, I'm taking a little piece of it with me in the form of a newly fashioned necklace made from a beach rock I found a few days ago.

We chose to visit Church of the Epiphany in South Haven, Michigan, in the context of *Boats without Oars* for a couple of reasons. The primary factor was that when the lay and ordained leaders of this small church learned about our project, they enthusiastically reached out and encouraged us to come. When we had contacted the Diocese of Western Michigan for a recommendation of churches in their area who were "doing interesting things with evangelism, showing signs of life," this was the parish suggested to us.

Photo: Kristin Carroccino. Enjoying the hospitality of Church of the Epiphany, South Haven, Michigan. July 2012.

Church of the Epiphany is a small but vibrant community, growing steadily after a very difficult church split in which at least 70 percent of the members left to form a new Anglican church around five years ago. "I was a stranger and you welcomed me in," is a phrase that came to mind yesterday as we joined the parish for Sunday worship. Sight unseen, this community had arranged our lodging in a parishioner's home, scheduled meals, conversations, and interviews with us, and had even hosted a birthday dinner for Michael and me on the evening we arrived. During the Sunday service, we learned that one family had opened their home to a man just released from the emergency room at the local hospital with no other place to go. Epiphany has recently begun holding burial services for the unclaimed remains of people left at the local mortuary, permanently giving them a final resting place in their memorial garden. This congregation of about thirty also offers building space for a yoga class, a few different recovery programs, and an adult community education program for students hoping to earn their GED. Epiphany considers all of these programs' attendees to be part of the parish.

The people at Church of the Epiphany are radically welcoming, not as a new outreach idea, but because so many of them have received deep hospitality. Most church members we have spoken with arrived at Epiphany in the last few years from diverse faith traditions—Catholic, Reformed, Jewish. All are truly welcome here. The warmth is contagious and inviting, and we feel reluctant to leave. However, Mirella has a birthday to celebrate tomorrow along the shores of Lake Superior, so we pack up our new beach rocks and drive north.

Photo: Kristin Carroccino. On the shore of Lake Michigan near South Haven, Michigan, July 2012.

God Isn't Waiting on Us to Get Our Act Together. *Michael*

"It has been my experience that God is present and most effective when we are at our most desperate. . .When all else fails we get interested in spiritual things," says Rector Michael Ryan, describing his initial interest in coming to Church of the Epiphany in South Haven, Michigan. He arrived in 2009—almost two years after a devastating church split—to find a core group of less than twenty. He and the remaining parishioners began working to ascertain what might be the next steps for their church. They called on the expertise of Rev. Tom Brackett, the Episcopal Church's Missioner for Church Planting and Ministry Redevelopment. Rev Brackett told Epiphany they had essentially two options: "he said we could decide to trust that God was longing for this community to do good things, and start listening and trying to discern what that was, OR we could decide to treasure our memories, keep doing what we'd always done, and move intentionally toward the process of dying. Either way, there was a lot of dying to do." The decision from the leadership team? "Bring on the dying that we need to do, so that we can move forward and participate in the good things that God is already doing in our community."

That decision set the tone for what is now a vibrant and unique church presence in South Haven. While Epiphany's Sunday attendance remains steady, the number of people who interact with and contribute to the church on a regular basis has increased dramatically. During the week, the building serves as host to a number of yoga classes and an adult education program, and the church works hard to make all of them feel that they are a part of the community.

In his first few months, Fr. Michael began to offer a Centering Prayer group hoping to generate interest among parishioners, but was surprised when a varied but faithful group with a more Eastern mindset joined him instead. The yogis already using the building were the first visitors. Over time, this group blossomed into a variety of offerings, including a widely attended book group exploring spiritual titles. Even people who never attend Sunday worship take part in other ministries and offerings of the church. How did this transformation take place?

In the early stages of their recovery from the church's split, the leadership team utilized a model of discernment based on Peter Block's book *Community: The Structure of Belonging* that fostered an atmosphere of deep mutual trust and spiritual exploration. Team members were so moved by these meaningful conversations, they decided to share them with a larger community. They invited over ninety people from the neighborhood, and with the group who responded, (about half of whom were not "members") leaders facilitated the same series of deep small-group discussions. The people who participated in the "knee-to-knee" conversations were energized by the experience.

"We already had all the vitality we needed to be the church we wanted to be; we didn't need any more people. We wanted more, and that's a good thing, but we already had everything we needed to get going." Epiphany readily accepted their South Haven neighbors, and even invited the people from yoga and Centering Prayer to attend the annual parish retreat. The parish's open invitation had tremendous effects: at the time of our visit, almost half of the budget came from people who didn't attend Epiphany on Sundays, but who loved what the church was doing and considered themselves part of the community.

Early in his tenure, Fr. Michael realized there was a strong disconnect between the church's worship and its community life. In a room designed for a much larger crowd, the twenty who attended weekly sat far apart. "We were worshiping with the ghosts of the people who used to be here, and probably with some small longing that 'maybe they'll come back.'" Something needed to change, so Fr. Michael did something he says "they tell you never to do." He rearranged the furniture and changed the worship time. As a result, the church lost its music director, choir (the majority of whom continued to attend worship), and most of the pews.

In its new location below the opening of the chancel rail, the Communion table has become the central feature in this ecumenical worship space. Behind the altar, on the raised platform where the table once stood, there is now a circle of cushions and chairs for the Centering Prayer group. In front of the Communion table are the pews, in rows that face one another across a central aisle. People now sit close to one another, even sharing hymnals and bulletins. "For the first time," said a longtime member "we can see each others' eyes." Rearranging the worship space blurred previous community barriers, so that congregants feel more connected.

Fr. Michael successfully made these remarkable changes, which more fully reflected the community's experience of discernment, while still maintaining an unapologetically Christian identity. Parishioners began to see and celebrate God at work in unexpected places and felt no pressure to grow the church or duplicate what it once was. One community member told me:

This congregation, by virtue of its recent history, recognizes that it has to participate in the community and be open to the community in ways that most comfortably situated churches don't see the need and therefore are dying. That's the story of Epiphany: there's the book club, there's yoga, there's some Buddhists in there, there's just an open closeness without any of that clingy, I-wonder-if-you're-going-to-join-my-church-and-come-every-Sunday kind of feel. You'd think that a church like this would be very anxious, and I'm sure that some are, but I don't feel it.

Epiphany found that being open to new ideas after a devastating church split was revitalizing. The more porous their walls became, the more life they discovered. On the inside of the front doors at Church of the Epiphany, a sign states "Let 'em wonder what's going on at Epiphany." Judging by my experience in this community, I'm sure that many people in South Haven are doing exactly that. During my interviews, no one told me stories about the past, but about the present. Openly embracing life and all those who visit, Church of the Epiphany truly offers hope to its community, which is thriving because of that most basic Christian principle: resurrection.

Photos: Kristin Carroccino. From top: Niagara Falls; World's tallest buffalo, Jamestown, South Dakota; Sandhill crane, Lake Superior; Art from the backseat; Our campsite in Stanislaus National Forest, California.

A Sense of Place: St Luke's in Fort Yates on the Standing Rock Indian Reservation, North Dakota. *Kristin*

The Standing Rock Indian Reservation occupies a remote expanse of land in an already sparsely populated state. We drove south toward its northern border from Bismarck, after having dinner with Canon John Floberg, Deacon Sloane Floberg, their family, and a group of volunteers from St. Paul's Episcopal Church in Philadelphia. Endless fields of green and gold, radiant in the setting sun, rushed past our car. Bales of hay and large farm machines dotted the landscape. Thousands of dragonflies and grasshoppers darted at us, startled by our passing car, which caused Michael to swerve every couple of minutes to avoid the onslaught. After about a half hour of driving, we made a couple of turns and found ourselves at Camp Gabriel, our sleeping quarters for the next few days. Our welcome sign was an old yellow school bus with the painted words "Episcopal Diocese of North Dakota" being slowly weathered away by the constant prairie winds.

Camp Gabriel was being readied for summer, when groups of local (Standing Rock) teenagers come to spend three-day sessions swimming, hanging out, and talking about Jesus with the volunteers, several of whom partner with the para-church group YoungLife. We arrived just before sunset with a list of instructions about where to find the toilet, how to turn on the lights, and the location of spare bed linens. We unloaded supplies the Flobergs sent with us: sacks full of boxed cereal, bags of chips, and groceries to feed us and the three or four teenage boys and Fr. Emmanuel from Philadelphia for a couple of days. Around us loomed a few weathered buildings containing beds, a kitchen, and camping equipment. A pool and basketball court anchored the campus with its dry earth and constantly blowing breeze. Meadowlarks atop fence posts sang and signaled the end of the day. We finished unpacking and settled in for an evening of listening to the rattle of loose boards and mice scampering overhead.

During our time on the Reservation, we were busy: we interviewed ministers and volunteers, learned more about the YoungLife partnership with the Episcopal Church in this diocese, drove to the "Agency" town of Ft. Yates, where we conducted interviews and attended church. Ft. Yates supports the Standing Rock offices, the Bureau of Indian affairs, displays the original "standing rock" on a pillar, and the first burial site of the famous Lakota chief Sitting Bull. After driving past the rock and the burial site, we spent a few hours listening to stories from several of the Lakota elders who attend and serve at St. Luke's, one of three small Episcopal churches on the Reservation. These churches date back to the days when missionaries from various denominations were given permission by the U.S. Government to move onto Reservations and provide services, which included churches, boarding schools, and other types of aid. This part of U.S. history— Native American children forcibly sent to boarding schools and often punished for speaking their native languages and of native culture being suppressed by the federal government—is painful to grapple with, and as a white outsider, I felt constantly aware of this history and its continuing effects on the people I saw and interviewed.

Photo credit: Kristin Carroccino. St. Luke's Episcopal Church, Ft. Yates. Standing Rock Reservation. July 2012.

I was surprised to learn about Episcopal churches being dominant on Indian Reservations in North and South Dakota, and initially assumed that Anglican missionaries had been the first to evangelize this territory. Like so much of Native American history in the United States, the truth is far more complicated and discouraging. Under the Quaker plan, which was federal policy between 1874 and 1890, each Native American nation was "assigned" a different Christian denomination, such that in the far western states, the Baptists were assigned to the Crow, the Presbyterians to the Nez Perce, and the Episcopalians to the Lakota Nation. While surely many missionaries had pure motives and Christian zeal, ultimately, the church meted out the same abuses as the federal government toward Native peoples. Martin Brokenleg, a member of the Lakota Nation and Episcopal priest for many decades describes this disheartening history:

> Christianity entered the lives of Native people as an accomplice to the military, political, and cultural forces. Those forces irrevocably altered life as previously known on this continent. Missionaries came with soldiers and government officials. The message of Jesus faded against the blast of cultural change. For Native young people, indoctrination and psychological abuse in schools included memorizing catechisms and kneeling in church. Massacres of entire Native communities stained the Christian

reputation of the soldiers and officers. The Christian faith, as introduced to Native people, is not clean.[20]

Michael, the children, and I were welcomed into two different Lakota homes during our visit to Standing Rock. One of the women, Delores, is an ordained deacon who serves primarily at St. Luke's; her husband is a retired laborer. The couple traveled across the U.S. for decades, following his jobs working on power lines, railways, and oil fields. Both husband and wife enjoyed telling stories, though Delores was more relatable and easier to understand. They are mostly retired, and enjoying that life. Delores takes her ministry very seriously, and cares deeply about the Episcopal Church and its presence on the Reservation.

Several generations of her family grew up in the local church, and relatives are buried near Camp Gabriel. Delores talked some about Native spirituality and the ongoing suspicion most Lakota feel toward Christianity. She said that church attendance is down, that the current trend is for many people she knows to practice the Native religion, attending sun dances and pipe ceremonies. This worries her.

Though the Episcopal Church today on Standing Rock is inclusive of many Native traditions and practices, the trend is for tribal members to remain skeptical and often antagonistic about church. Both Deacon Delores and Canon Floberg tell us, that despite this collective cynicism, the priest and deacon are often called out to pray for the sick or to attend middle-of-the-night crises with Lakota who refuse to attend church, but have parents and grandparents who were faithful Episcopalians.

The other woman we visited was Delores' soft-spoken niece. She attends church, but not as frequently as her aunt does. Her home is tidy, and she has a car and a decent job, and a husband (or boyfriend) currently in jail. She has a few cats that fascinated our children, and she gladly obliged the kids' requests for slices of white bread that they spied in a bright plastic bag on her kitchen counter. I spent my time at her home mostly keeping my increasingly restless kids entertained while she talked with Michael and Delores.

---

[20] Martin Brokenleg. "That the People may Live: a Native American History," http://www.augie.edu/dept/nast/Projects/doc1.htm. This essay recounting a partial history of Native Americans and church is long but fascinating and thoughtfully explains the different way ministers much preach to and interact with Native people in relation to Christianity because of wounds inflicted by the church in the past and because of the great differences between European and Native Americans spirituality.

On Sunday, we worshiped together at St. Luke's. Father John gave the announcements; Deacons Sloane and Delores led the music, read the Gospel, sent us out with a blessing; Michael preached with our daughter wrapped around his legs and refusing to move; Father Emmanuel from Philadelphia presided over the Eucharist; all of us knelt and shared the common meal. After the service, the congregation hosted a potluck meal for us. I felt unsure of myself as I sat with a few of the women; most of the men ate separately. During the church service, a visibly drunk man was escorted in by two friends or relatives. We learned that he had been released just that morning from the hospital and had pleaded to be taken to church. Given the lack of surprise among those gathered, this wasn't unusual. He snored and talked loudly, then began coughing, and was eventually led back out of the building by his companions. Between Mirella hanging onto Michael during his sermon and worshipping in a small congregation that included a very ill and inebriated man, I was completely at a loss for how to interact. My deep Southern roots that bestowed the gift of social small talk when necessary, and my more recently acquired northwestern openness were not helping me in this complicated-feeling society.

So, I sat respectfully, and ate, enjoyed the hospitality, and listened to a few of the women gossip in the Lakota language. I've spent enough time in Navajo land to know this is probably the best course of action. Soon, the women began engaging me in their stories, and I heard many accounts of hard living. The statistics we read or hear about regarding life on Reservations just scratches the surface of the ongoing troubles many Native Americans encounter: repeated arrests, alcohol and drug abuse, teenage pregnancies. Eventually, one of the women's stories allowed me the opportunity to segue into a few questions about their own lives. It became clear, as in some other Native cultures, that the women, especially the grandmothers, are often the more resilient and reliable of the sexes.

I was stunned and saddened to hear stories of how recently these women have experienced racial hatred and persecution. One woman recounted taking her daughter, maybe a decade ago, to a shopping mall in Bismarck to buy new shoes. The staff blatantly ignored both mother and daughter when they asked for help. No other customers were in the store, and this woman's young daughter clearly knew which shoes she wanted her mother to buy for her. The store clerks refused to sell the shoes, and asked the woman to leave. The mother later returned (or called) and confronted the manager, who apologized. These are still fresh and too-common memories for my Lakota acquaintances.

Though I had said little and offered nothing more than my family's presence on this hot Sunday, the women were delighted by my company and seemed glad to have related some of their complicated histories to me. I was honored to hear them, but it was time to gather the children and depart. I began to develop a dull headache brought on by this foreign experience. Michael was gathering his things to leave, having offered to do a few hours' work back at Camp Gabriel before our departure. As we started to say our good-byes and thanks, the deacon and one of her friends told me they had a gift for us, since we were guests, and handed us a "star quilt" wall hanging, a symbol of hospitality in the community. Aside from reflexive motions of gratitude on my part, I felt speechless again. Poverty and loss are so apparent on Standing Rock, but gifts are freely given. We were clearly the outsiders, but were openly welcomed.

The heat and the winds grew increasingly intense later in the afternoon at Camp Gabriel, and having received the stories we needed for our project, we decided to continue our journey north and west one day early. We left Standing Rock with many things to think about, and received many blessings, one of the greatest being watching such a small group of people in a rarely visited corner of the world feed and care for each other and welcome us with big, warm hearts.

Photo: Kristin Carroccino. Camp Gabriel, Standing Rock Reservation, North Dakota. July 2012.

The Best of Both Worlds. *Michael*

I'm standing with Canon John Floberg outside North Dakota's Camp Gabriel, and the blistering, 100-degree air is blowing past us at roughly forty miles per hour, buffeting our hair and clothes with its withering heat. An hour ago, John was chopping down the camp's unruly grass ("sometimes we get rattlesnakes") with a riding lawn mower, yet he is still wearing his clergy shirt—sans collar—from this morning's worship. He's just given me a ten-minute history of the Episcopal Church's involvement with the Lakota/Dakota/Nakota people, from hospitals and soup kitchens to boarding schools. With such a complex cultural and political history, John says the Standing Rock Reservation "forces you to become pastoral really quickly, or else you leave."

Ministry on the Standing Rock Indian Reservation requires an almost wholly different skill set than any place we have visited on our travels. The people here are among the most committed Episcopalians I have met; many of them are only a generation removed from the tribe's first Christians. There is little concern among parishioners regarding the nebulous future of mainline Christianity in America: instead, the whole of the church's energy is directed at providing for the spiritual, physical, and psychological needs of people who straddle two very different worlds. When I asked about how the church fits into people's lives here, interviewees talked to me about clothing, food, and shelter. They alluded to tragedy, poverty, racism, and their worries for their children and grandchildren far and near. The church is their solace and their support network, the place where they find people who share their joys and sorrows, and the place where they lift up both needs and blessings in devoted prayer.

The three tiny Episcopal churches on the Reservation are all deeply committed to Standing Rock's youth population. John started building Camp Gabriel for youth over fifteen years ago, and soon he was approached by YoungLife to form a partnership in youth ministry. This resulted in an active presence by the Episcopal Church throughout the reservation, with two ordained deacons working full time in youth ministry. I spoke at length to both of the deacons, and their passion for mentoring young people and watching them succeed was clear in the animation and energy of their stories. Each week, school-age youth are bused in from several small towns on the reservation to attend one of several YoungLife club meetings, and Camp Gabriel runs several sessions every summer. In a place where young people often feel hopeless, the churches are working hard to provide a loving environment and display the hope of the Gospel.

The unique identity of being both Native and Christian asserts itself in a variety of ways, and for the people I talked to, it is this very identity which holds them together through thick and thin. The Sunday liturgy flows from English to Dakota and back, and the design of the worship incorporates a variety of native symbolism. I heard stories of cultural juxtaposition that left my head spinning: tobacco offerings and soup kitchens, clergy conferences and smudges, Prayers of the People and Sun Dances. Navigating between the cultures—especially given their shared history—is a theologically complex and sometimes touchy area of church life, and it is a constantly evolving dance.

Not long before our visit, Canon John participated in a rite for the restoration of sacred objects after being profaned; a reference to the church's sad history of devaluing native art and culture. During one infamous 19th-century clergy conference, the bishop demanded the immediate removal all native-influenced liturgical decorations and objects. The items were sealed in a barrel and carted away, never to be seen again. In this year's clergy conference, the restoration rite took place as priests rolled a barrel into the midst of the gathering and opened it to reveal a newly commissioned buffalo hide "winter count," depicting seventy-two stories from the Gospel of Luke, which they consecrated for use in the church as a sacred text.

Canon Floberg is well aware of missteps made by the church in the past, yet keeps them in the context of a broader story: the church originally came to Standing Rock in part because no one else was working to counteract the horrific conditions of natives on reservations. On his wall at home, John keeps several paintings of Twelfth-Century Norwegian stave churches. They remind him to take a long view of his work. He says, "the first missionaries arrived in [Scandinavian countries] in the Ninth Century, and these churches represent the first truly Norwegian expression of Christianity. It took three hundred years." To wit, he observes drily, "the church has only been on the reservation for about a hundred and fifty." John's ministry is part of the painstakingly long process of discovering a truly acculturated expression of Christianity, and success is measured in small—and very pastoral—steps.

A Community of Truth. *Kevin Goodrich*

A reality in North Dakota is that we cannot rely upon Episcopalians moving into town to sustain our churches. This is a growing trend for all denominations across North America as Christianity declines and denominational loyalty continues to weaken. However, this is especially true in a sparsely populated rural state whose Christian heritage is mostly Catholic and Lutheran. This means we have to consider what we have to offer to the dechurched and unchurched beyond our denominational identity. We have to consider: what is it that people need?

People need community. Sometimes Christians define evangelism in ways that are highly individualistic, as if evangelism were only about an individual and their relationship with God. Archbishop William Temple provides a more robust understanding of evangelism in his classic definition, "evangelism is the presentation of Jesus Christ in the power of the Holy Spirit, in such ways that persons may be led to believe in him as Savior and follow him as Lord within the fellowship of his Church." Human beings were created for community. They will seek it out in any way they can find it. They will even accept unhealthy community in lieu of having none. As churches we can offer people healthy community, community rooted in the love of Jesus Christ (1 John 4:7-12).

People also need truth. Many churches are friendly. Seekers are able to find warm friendships, connections with individuals of multiple generations (this is increasingly a treasure for many people who don't have strong family ties or who are living far away from their biological families), and caring support during life's highs and lows. However, many of these same churches are not places where the truth of the Gospel is proclaimed and modeled in powerful and life-changing ways. Evangelism doesn't happen unless an individual encounters the person of Jesus Christ and makes a choice to follow Him (Matthew 4:18-19). You can grow a church without truth, but in that case, you are making church members not disciples.

Grace Church in Jamestown, North Dakota, is a small congregation that has been revitalized by a commitment to developing a community where people are welcomed, and by developing a community where the truth of the Gospel is proclaimed and lived. The church has embraced an open attitude which says that, "Doubts are OK, questions are welcomed, please, come as you are." The combination of warm fellowship, an openness to the struggles that people find themselves in (addiction, atheism, broken relationships, etc.), and a commitment to the basic truths of the Christian faith have resulted in many unchurched and dechurched persons connecting with Christ and the Church.

It's not that denominational identity is not of value. Our Episcopal identity shapes our community and our commitment to truth in a particular way. The mistake in our post-Christian society is to assume that a denominational identity will be an effective tool for evangelism by itself; it won't. However, combined with a healthy community and a healthy commitment to the basic truths of the Gospel, denominational identity can be part of the package the Holy Spirit uses to draw people to Himself (John 6:44).

Fr. Kevin Goodrich, O.P. is a Canon Missioner in the Episcopal Diocese of North Dakota and a life-professed member of the Anglican Order of Preachers (Dominicans). He regularly writes and teaches about evangelism. His blog is: http://anglicandominican.blogspot.com/.

Good Medicine. *Kristin*

In the Bighorn Mountains of Wyoming, Caedmon was ill for the first time during our travels. He laid in the tent, feverish, while Michael set up a camp kitchen in a remote area where we had decided to rest for a few days and visit the Native American sacred site, the Medicine Wheel. Caedmon woke fever-free with lots of energy the following morning, and the day after that watched moose grazing a few hundred feet away as we packed up our tent. The only other illness we encountered during *Boats without Oars* was short, but dramatic: a bout of stomach flu shared by Michael and me in a hotel room in Clanton, Alabama, the night before our interview with Fr. Bill King of Trinity Episcopal Church. We arrived at the interview the next morning, pale and limp after a mostly sleepless night involving alternate sprints to the cold bathroom toilet. In addition, Michael acquired a bruised rib a half hour prior to our meeting with Fr. Bill, as he wrenched the trunk of the car closed with that last, final shove of anger. Such fits of frustration over how things could (mostly) fit in the trunk one day and not the next, thus leading to another rearranging of our life support system for the summer (tent, food, clothes) soon led to the wisdom that Michael was best left alone to fight the demon trunk.

Illness, weather, and traveling with small children thwart many well-made vacation plans. By God's grace, our illnesses were few, and minor, and we only spent one night in a campground in North Carolina worried about nearby tornados. However, we absolutely spent a lot of time with our two small children in the car. When asked by skeptical parents how we managed to "keep the kids entertained" over all of the miles, I usually just shrug my shoulders. In general, we kept to a routine and adopted the mindset that our home was where we were together, whether it was in a host family's guest room, hotel, or campground. We also swept the children up into our adventure by reading books ahead of time about the places we planned to tour, and we made a three-ringed binder for each of them that had a different section for each state we hoped to visit. Both children became "junior rangers" in a few different national parks. And, admittedly, they had a few thousand miles of road trips under their car-seat belts prior to *Boats without Oars*. Mostly, though, they devised their own games and stories to keep themselves company.

Mirella, for example, spent many of her days creating adventures for "Wanda," a small porcelain-headed and -handed colonial girl doll she brought to us with wide, pleading eyes in the gift shop at Plimoth Plantation, Massachusetts. Wanda got rigged into a ribbon harness and raised and lowered over the little plastic attachment on the grab-handle meant to hold clothes hangers. On one particular day, Wanda and many other small and sundry items flowed out of the car onto the pavement of the Ben & Jerry's ice cream factory parking lot near Stowe, Vermont. We had arrived to take

a tour and eat free ice cream. The deluge of miscellaneous items and

Photo: Kristin Carroccino. Mirella and "Wanda" in Vermont. June 2012.

growing mountain of coloring books, travel brochures, and leaky water bottles began to cause me extreme mental anguish. No amount of bribing or threats convinced the children to "put things back where you found them" or "please don't start something new until you've finished the last thing." Even the prospect of a visit from the ominous "clean-up fairy," who might just take items and keep them indefinitely until things get tidier, didn't persuade our brood to change their ways. Instead, they devised traps to catch the sprite that made nightly visits and created another bag of flotsam for Michael to find room for in the trunk of the car.

By the time we reached Wyoming's Bighorn Mountains and Caedmon's feverish

night, none of us could easily recollect our "normal" life back at the Seminary in Austin. We had grown accustomed to the simplicity and rhythm of camping life and become more open and accommodating to meeting new people in all kinds of situations. Mirella had celebrated her 5th birthday by blowing out a candle on a cupcake in a hotel room on the shores of Lake Superior in Michigan. Michael and I

Photo: Kristin Carroccino. Caedmon, packed in.

celebrated our birthdays in a tiny "Kamping Kabin" at a KOA campground near Indianapolis with crusty bread, wine, and local cheese and strawberries. Caedmon, a lover of spacecraft technology, had met Charlie Bolden, the director of NASA, at a worship service in Washington, D.C. Our expectations and preconceptions continued to be challenged: about ourselves, our family life, what "comfort" means, and about church.

The morning Caedmon woke fever-free, we hiked up to the Medicine Wheel, playing the "quiet game" of trying to tread in silence (largely unsuccessfully), until we crested the ridge and the wheel came into view. We chose stones at the foot of the mountain and carried them with us; my rock was about the size of my fist, and square. As we hiked, my focus cleared, and I heard ravens, noticed tiny, tenacious flowers growing out of rock. Then, I felt sudden, unexpected anger and the urge to throw my rock. I held it and knew I would lay it down along with my anger at the Medicine Wheel. We summited and were silenced by the whipping wind and sight of tattered prayer flags waving the petitions of their owners up toward the cobalt sky. A volunteer reminded us that this was sacred holy ground and to enter it respectfully.

Native Americans have come to this hallowed place for hundreds of years to seek guidance and healing. In its presence, we were mindful of and thankful for the insight, healing, and good medicine this around-the-U.S. journey had provided so far for us. The kids left stick and grass offerings on one of the rocks that form a wheel spoke; I placed my stone and residual anger close by, and we left reverentially, and full.

Photo: Kristin Carroccino. Medicine Wheel, Big Horn Mountains, Wyoming. July 2012.

A Sense of Place: Epiphany Parish and Seattle. *Kristin*

We have reached Seattle and Epiphany Parish, the site of our seventh and final official church visit for *Boats without Oars*.

This is also a homecoming, a return to the Diocese of Olympia, which has been supporting Michael through the ordination process for Episcopal priests. We feel at home here, oddly excited to be wearing sweaters on chilly July evenings and donning slippers to wear around the small apartment offered by one of Epiphany's parishioners for a few days. Aside from conducting interviews and spending time with Epiphany's community, we plan to be Seattle tourists and visit Seattle Center to ride the monorail, wander around Pike Place Market with our friend Kimberly, and spend as much time as we can in city parks enjoying the cool weather and green trees.

We became Episcopalians in this diocese, and spending a few days at Epiphany Parish, situated comfortably between downtown Seattle and Lake Washington, felt both invigorating and comfortable. Our Bishop, Greg Rickel, suggested that we visit Epiphany Parish to explore a church that is growing quickly, and one that is quite different demographically from the other six churches we have visited this

Photo: Public Domain. Epiphany Parish, Seattle.

summer. Epiphany is located in a typical, upper middle-class Seattle neighborhood with steep hills and tall houses, no two looking anything alike. Locals know that the end of July and early August are the "best" times to visit Seattle, when veils of flowers in rainbow colors spill over planter boxes and creep over curbs, the skies are mostly blue, and the weather is sublime. Epiphany's neighborhood offers most of Seattle's trademarks: dogs, strollers, and cyclists are abundant, and verdant views abound. What makes a Seattle neighborhood truly excellent is at least one good "walk-able" coffee shop, and though I didn't see one in the block surrounding the church, I'm sure there must be one close by.

When we arrived at Epiphany to meet the Rector and conduct interviews, a brigade of women carrying clippers was bustling about in the church gardens, gathering flowers to prepare the altar for Sunday services. One of the gardeners paused to direct us to the office of Father Doyt Conn, Epiphany's priest for almost four years. Doyt's office was warm and comfortable, and like the offices of many priests, overflowing with books. He was friendly and direct, enthusiastic to begin our conversation, and to offer generous hospitality. He took time in our flurry of introductions to point out to our children a gecko that resides in a small aquarium on one of the bookshelves. Then, he gave us a tour of the church grounds.

Michael and I got Caedmon and Mirella settled into a colorful preschool room filled with beautiful toys, then we sat on polished tree stumps in one of the preschool's playgrounds and got to know Fr. Doyt and the story of Epiphany. Rev. Doyt is a quick and engaging conversationalist, and asked us as many questions as we posed to him. In a large parish comprised of many double career, white-collar families, which is growing quickly, Fr. Doyt's energy seems to be a good match. Later in the evening, our family had dinner at Fr. Doyt's home along with three other couples with children close in age to ours. It was an ideal Seattle evening: cool breezes, fresh food, good wines, and robust conversation interrupted with excursions to check on the locations of the children.

On Sunday morning, Michael preached and shared our *Boats without Oars* story at Epiphany's two Sunday morning services. The liturgy was precise and rich, the music outstanding, and the pews were mostly full. Episcopal churches in Western Washington on beautiful Sunday mornings in August usually have low attendance. Epiphany is clearly a community that engenders parishioners' participation and loyalty. When the kids and I hurried into the nave five minutes late, the organ was already pumping out the chords of a lively hymn, and everyone I passed on my way to the few remaining seats (in the front row, of course) was heartily singing. I was curious to know if Epiphany's' attendees are always so joyfully engaged. What drives this level of participation?

After the church service, we attended the coffee hour for a few minutes, and I noticed that far fewer people were there compared to those gathered for worship earlier in the nave. Not knowing anyone and remembering the three playgrounds to choose from around Epiphany's campus, we ducked out to look for other families by the playscapes. I recognized two of the children and their parents at the playground closest to our car, and we adults stood and made small talk while the kids burned off pent up energy from sitting in church then eating cookies at coffee hour. Our casual conversation soon turned to a discussion about parenting and praying with our children. Michael and I were continually endeavoring to find regular bedtime prayers that held the kids' attention and our patience.

These new acquaintances told us that they prayed the office of Compline each night with their two children, who are similar in age to Caedmon and Mirella. For at least a year, they had nightly used the thin, black *Hour by Hour* prayer book. The prayers are succinct, but offer a psalm, verse, and shortened versions of prayers from the *Book of Common Prayer*. Their kids had learned that this was part of the family's routine, and praying Compline had become a habit. I loved the idea of trying this at home. When we returned to Epiphany the next day for Michael's final interviews, I was delighted when the father of this family gave me a copy of the book. These trim books are available to all parishioners, and now I began to see that the enthusiastic participation in Sunday worship probably reflected a much deeper, daily prayer practice among Epiphany's parishioners. Over the next few days, Michael and I began to introduce Compline to our children. (Update: more than two years later, this is still part of our almost-nightly practice; we pray Compline in some form most nights, usually from *Hour by Hour*.)

What strikes me most about spending a couple of days with this community is that the energy is palpable; there is genuine enthusiasm about the dramatic growth that has been happening at Epiphany in the last three years, and strong evidence of a church that places high value on individual and corporate spiritual practices. I left the nave after the Sunday service feeling grateful for the wide variety of church communities we have been able to worship with this summer, each unique from all of the others. We have sung hymns and prayed with Christians from incredibly diverse cultures across the U.S., and I have seen many different expressions of encountering God. All of these experiences are strengthening my faith.

A Church You would Invite Your Friends to See. *Michael*

Fr. Doyt Conn repeatedly refers to himself as a broken record: "I don't know if I've told you this already, but I say the same things over and over again." He does, and it seems to be working. I met Fr. Doyt in April 2012 at a clergy conference, where he made a strong impression on me: in a room full of priests who had been asked to share what they were doing to grow their churches, Rev. Doyt stood up and announced to the gathering that he had grown his church—Epiphany Parish in Seattle—by doing the same old thing again and again every Sunday. And it has grown—fantastically—by every measure: people are flocking to Epiphany to take part in the "same old thing" that has somehow been made new.

Nearly everyone I interviewed at Epiphany was quick to mention that Sunday worship is an integral part of his or her faith. This church's approach to Sunday services is just what you would expect from a broken record: they are very consistent. The servers and acolytes know exactly what they are doing and when, the priests know their liturgy well, and practice their sermons weekly, and the people in the congregation don't hesitate to say or sing their parts in the liturgy. On the Sunday we attended Epiphany's services, when my attention briefly wandered near the end of the offertory music, I looked at the nearby servers; their eyes were fixed on the musician playing the piano. Fr. Doyt arrived at Epiphany with a vision of liturgy that was "precise without being fussy," and created a climate where training is thorough and Saturday rehearsals for Sunday services are common. There is even a verger (a person who assists in ordering church services) on staff, and she draws from a broad pool of volunteers in her weekly planning. The people at Epiphany Parish love their liturgy, and they participate fully, no matter what role they are filling.

In almost every interview, parishioners referenced traditional spiritual practices, and their language suggested that these grew out of their experience at Epiphany. One man told me about reading Compline every night to his kids, two or three mentioned their upcoming pilgrimage, and I even heard a mention or two of fasting. When I asked Fr. Doyt to explain, he held up seven fingers: "Daily prayer, weekly worship, Sabbath time, liturgical seasons, pilgrimage, fasting, and tithing," he said, are the central practices of our faith. As you might expect by now, Fr. Conn constantly mentions these practices in his writing and sermons as the mode by which people can cultivate spiritual growth. His efforts have created a common language for Epiphany's parishioners to discuss their spiritual lives, and empowered them to strike their own balance among the variety of practices. Before the end of our four-day visit, someone gave Kristin a copy of *Hour by Hour*, a book of Daily Office prayers shared freely among the congregation to unite them in their prayer lives. Epiphany Parish challenges people to live into a very distinct and very traditional way of Christian discipleship.

I heard the phrase, "holy ground" quite often; this church is striving to be a sacred and peaceful space in their neighborhood. Epiphany's well-manicured gardens and patios brighten the campus. Their carillon plays hymns several times daily. There are preschool children everywhere during the week, and there is work underway to make a drop-in public space for meeting friends, sitting quietly, or using the wireless network. Epiphany's campus is a lively and magnetic place, and the parishioners here hope that their church grounds can serve as a place of respite (or even transformation) for all who are passing through.

The people of Epiphany are finding something unique in a world of ubiquitous change and uncertainty: a place where they can commit their lives to a community that is doing Kingdom work. In being unflinchingly Episcopalian, tirelessly consistent, and openly welcoming, this church is providing its members with a strong sense of identity and mission in both their individual spiritual lives and their shared religious practice. Parishioners are pursuing discipleship with the goal of creating transformation in the world around them, or as one interviewee said, "getting sucked up in the wake of what Jesus is already doing." Because of this transformative presence, these parishioners are surprisingly committed to their church. They give generously of their time and resources, and they claim ownership in nearly every aspect of parish life. From pastoral care and prayer chains to formation and children's programming, someone—if not a team of people—is dedicated to ensuring its success.

All of this comes together seamlessly on any given Sunday to present a worship service that is at once inspiring and accessible. The music program is top-notch, attracting even non-Christians to participate in the choir. Although the singers were on summer break, the congregation was enthusiastic and voluble; and I suspect that if I were to return on any other Sunday I would experience similar energy. Epiphany's consistency may indeed appear to be a broken record, but broken records, it seems, can create beautiful music.

Spiritual Practices. *Michael Yankoski*

"[Aren't] spiritual practices kind of like trying to work our way to God?" I blurted out at last, struggling to find the right words. "You know, trying to make ourselves holy, or earning our own salvation, that sort of thing? Most days I have a hard enough time just keeping my head above water, and, to be honest, I don't have the strength to try and make God love me or even like me."

Father Solomon's face went grave, and he closed his eyes for several long moments. I wondered if I'd offended him somehow. When at last his response came, they were words of comfort, though the gravity of his tone shook the room like an earthquake, echoing in my soul like a song. "That's not the way this works, Michael," he said. "You needn't put that much faith in your own strength, for your strength is a mere atom beside an ocean of God's unending love. God is the Source. The Origin. The Ground of All Being. The One from whom and through whom and to whom are all things. You can't 'make God love you,' any more than you can *make* a star or planet or even a human being. Any more than you can make yourself."

I didn't respond but sat there in the silence, listening.

Father Solomon spoke again, and the shaking of my foundations continued. "The God who called you into existence *ex nihilio*—out of nothing—is the same God who holds you in existence this moment and every moment. Were he to withdraw his hand, you would vanish without memory. All things would. No, you can't *make* God love you. You can't make God *like* you. But nor do you need to; he already does. Never forget that is *why* he made you—because he *wants* you to exist. And not just exist. He wants you to *live life in all its fullness*."

When Father Solomon at last opened his eyes they were moist with tears, tears that coursed down into the deep wrinkles of his face, irrigating deserts as they went. But somehow these tears weren't embarrassing; I didn't look away but instead took in the monk's weathered old face and hoped—just for a moment—that what he was saying might actually be true. And in that moment, a warmth wrapped itself around me like a Caribbean breeze, so quick and fleeting that I wondered if I'd imagined it, but so evident that it left me breathless.

Father Solomon was talking again. "Spiritual practices are a way of mapping your own personal soulscape. Helping you become more acquainted with who you are, who God is, and the people he's placed you into this life alongside of."

"It's rather like sailing," he said. I thrilled at the thought of this monk out there on the open ocean, white hair billowing in the wind, drops of sea spray clinging to his whiskers. A veritable Old Man and the Sea.

"When you're sailing, you learn to be constantly attentive to the wind—how it is blowing over your sails, what direction it is coming from, how fast it is moving, that sort of thing. Does that make sense?"

I nodded.

"This attentiveness to the wind becomes the main task—no, that's not the right word—the main *art* of sailing. We must both attend to the wind and then *respond* to whatever it is that the wind is doing. We trim our sails, adjust our course, sometimes we even exchange one sail for another—whatever it takes so as to be in the most receptive place given what the wind is doing. Our attentiveness to the wind *allows the wind to move us.*"

"And spiritual practices are like that?" I asked. "Like adjusting our sails and making sure we're in a receptive place given what God is doing?"

"Exactly." Father Solomon was smiling as he spoke. "And—if you'll indulge me for a moment—this metaphor becomes all the more fascinating given that in Jesus' time there was only a single word for 'breath,' 'wind,' and 'spirit.' 'The Sprit of God,' 'The Breath of God,' and 'The Wind of God' are all accurate translations of a common New Testament phrase, a phrase that basically means *GET READY: God is up to something!*"

I fell silent, wondering what shape the sail of my soul might be, where it might take me if I allowed my Maker to set the course. Then I remembered something Father Solomon had said during our first meeting. "Interesting that you knew a 'storm' had brought me here to the monastery."

"Very interesting indeed," Father Solomon said with a smile. "Now the question is: How will you respond to what the Wind is doing in your life?"

This excerpt from The Sacred Year *is found on pages 12-14, and was printed with permission from Michael Yankoski's publisher, Thomas Nelson. This essay was added to* Boats without Oars *in 2014 and was not part of our 2012 blog.*

Michael Yankoski is a writer, aspiring theologian and urban homesteader who dreams of one day becoming a competent woodworker, musician, potter and sailor. He is the author of Under the Overpass *and also* The Sacred Year. *(www.TheSacredYear.com). He and his wife Danae are both PhD students at the University of Notre Dame. More of his work may be found at* www.MichaelYonkoski.com.

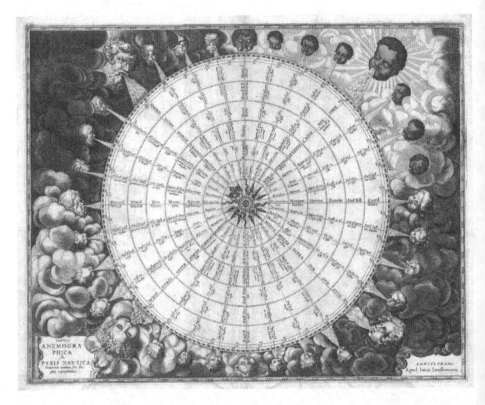

This image is a wind rose, more commonly known now as a "compass rose." Early forms of the compass rose were known as wind roses, because no differentiation was made between the cardinal direction and the wind that blew from that direction. North was often depicted with a fleur de lis, while east was pictured with a Christian cross, indicating the direction of Jerusalem from Europe.

Source: Wikimedia Commons. Artist: Jan Janssonius, Atlantis majoris quinta pars, orbem maritimum seu omnium marium orbis terrarium, *c. 1650.*

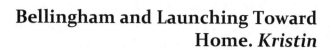

Bellingham and Launching Toward Home. *Kristin*

Bellingham spends more than half of her year cloaked in a foggy veil, which increases in varying intensity from a light drizzle in spring to freezing gusts in late autumn. Interspersed with varying shades of white and gray that swirl in the heavens are days of intense peacock-blue skies and sunbursts illuminating the Cascadian peaks of Mt. Baker and the Twin Sisters, giants who loom in the distance keeping watch over Bellingham Bay and its tiny white sailboats bobbing on the waves. It is a place of natural and personal drama, a thin strip of green between ocean and mountains, a landscape that demands soul searching and hones personalities that are both sharp and subtle. In this city of former loggers, educators, university students, anglers, artists, hikers, and foodies, we made our home for seven years. I love this place.

In Bellingham, Michael and I became Episcopalians, joining the community of St. Paul's, where we watched the church go through a painful split and begin to rebuild again. During that time, Michael discerned his call to the priesthood, I gave birth to both of our children, and we both spent a lot of time deeply listening to where God was working, and then listening a little more. We spent many hours walking among the cedars and Doug firs, letting the moss creep between our toes, imagining and creating our future.

Yesterday, Michael preached what will probably be the last sermon he will deliver as a layperson at our home congregation; this time next year, God willing, he will be ordained and beginning a job as a priest at a different church. That realization is bittersweet, a bit sad to be moving on from our sending church, but exhilarating to consider the possibilities and adventures ahead, even as we are on this great voyage of *Boats without Oars*.

I am thankful for these few days in Bellingham to be with friends, to sit at Jessica's table and drink her always-perfect, French press coffee and chat about how our children are growing. Michael and I went out on our second date of the summer (the first being long, long ago in Decatur, Alabama), while the kids reunited with their friends at "Parents' Night Out" courtesy of St. Paul's. After a long walk by Bellingham Bay, Michael and I savored wine and cheesecake with our own friends at a favorite restaurant. The conversation was energizing; our cohort was excited to hear about our findings concerning the Episcopal Church. One of our friends confided that he is in discernment for ordained ministry. We also had the opportunity to spend a few moments with our dear friend Frank, who was dying peacefully in his home, surrounded by his wife, daughters, softly playing classical music, and hospice workers.

What a summer it has been. Amazing. Now, we are headed south and eventually east and plan to spend the next few weeks meandering back to Austin and doing some deep listening, and integrating and reflecting on all of the many stories and experiences we have had over the last eleven weeks. I imagine that when we finally do arrive back at our driveway in Austin, we will feel like strangers—adventurers who have been to the wilds and now have to learn how to live again in the bustle and flow of the big city.

Photo: Kristin Carroccino. Bellingham Bay. August 2012.

Questions

Are "living out the Gospel" and "evangelism" synonymous?

What tensions (if any) result from asserting a strong Christian identity while openly welcoming and integrating newcomers into a community?

How can a church best accommodate its local culture without compromising its core Christian identity?

When a church's history includes painful stories, what are ways that the remaining community might honestly engage these stories while cultivating hope for the future?

How do good music, food, and programs help or hinder a church's evangelism?

AUGUST AND SEPTEMBER 2012: OUR DESTINATION IS WITHIN SIGHT

Thirteen Thousand Miles. *Kristin*

We have reached the thirteen-thousand mile and three-month mark of this long journey and are traveling now through the deserts and canyons of the American Southwest, a place where Michael and I lived when we were first married. These are the lands of deep reflection, of little water. The landscape feels alternately scarce and extravagant. When we lived in Moab, Utah, during the first year of our marriage, we each worked multiple jobs to make ends meet. In every moment we weren't working, we spent hours hiking through the harsh landscape to find hidden alcoves of shade, springs pouring from rocks, flowers bursting forth from sand, ancient Puebloan potsherds and red-stained hand prints left on sandstone walls. Those were days of beginning to find ourselves as adults and our place in the world apart from our familiar landscapes and families of origin. In the desert, we found abundance.

I imagine the ancient Celtic mariners on their coracles, though bobbing along on waves of the deep and cold oceans of the North Atlantic, found themselves in a "desert" as well. Having set off on a mission to find the abundance of God wherever they landed, they undoubtedly found life and abundance within themselves as they faced peril on the seas. New strength and creativity grew in places previously untapped. I also imagine that when they did land and offer their ministry to those who met them on distant shores, they often encountered unexpected and generous hospitality, a sort-of "reverse evangelism."

This summer, having left our comfortable home and familiar routines in Austin and set off not knowing what we would find along the way, one of the things I wasn't expecting to discover, and what gives me great hope for the future of the Episcopal Church, is the abundance of gifts and hospitality we have received along the way. From a photograph of our family posted on this website and a few e-mail exchanges, people heartily welcomed us into their homes and to their tables, excited to discuss their particular expression and experience of church. These were springs in the desert, wildflowers bursting forth from sand.

People offer hospitality each time we need extra funds or meals eaten out instead of cooked on the camp stove, or clean linens and a firm mattress. My understanding of abundance is expanding. Transformation doesn't usually happen without movement, a rule for life not limited, of course, to the individual, but groups of us forming churches and extending ourselves into unknown areas. This pursuit brings life and hope for the future of the Episcopal Church. Small acts of hospitality, like welcoming our family, expand into welcoming new communities, seeing new possibilities for where God is working.

Increasing flexibility is another life-giving, growing edge for me and for the church. I have seen this growth happening in our family over the summer when we have repeatedly faced days with no cell phone coverage or Internet connection. This particular deprivation limits our capacity to work on *Boats without Oars,* but creates hours of time to talk about and reflect upon our work, until we once again lodge in a place with modern technological connectivity. Faced with just a few ingredients for dinner because some food rotted in the heat of the car or the ice melted in the cooler sooner than expected, we have created new dishes that satisfied us more than when we were in Texas with a full kitchen and a plethora of markets from which to purchase food. As creativity has welled up from the need to be flexible with sometimes-limited options during our travels, I have been better able to recognize those communities who are thriving from their own capacity to be flexible and creative—to grow and bloom despite adverse circumstances, and to bear great fruit.

We have a few weeks of "desert time" left before returning to urban life in Austin, the rigors of Michael's academic schedule, my continuing attempts to find more time to write while homeschooling the kids, and the inevitable squall of details we will face. As we hike past hoodoos and look under clefts of rock for signs of life from ancient peoples in the next few days, we will be listening and watching for evidence of abundance, always there, but sometimes elusive at first glance. We will be slowing down to hear what further lessons we need to bring home with us to share.

This public domain image is of the "Four Evangelists" (Matthew, Mark, Luke, and John) from the Book of Kells.

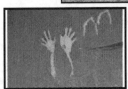

Photos: Kristin Carroccino. Top: return to Texas, Cadillac Ranch; middle: the miracle of making things fit in the car; bottom: Utah pictographs, Grand Canyon

Journal Entries. August 4-7. Big Meadow Campground, Stanislaus National Forest, California.
Kristin

August 4.

We are in a place for three nights with no goal other than to rest and maybe drive thirty minutes to hike around in giant Sequoia trees. This is a dusty but pleasant place so far. Slow moving insects occasionally crawl around the tent; a dragonfly enters, stares at us, and then departs. The hammock hangs between two Ponderosa Pines. Caedmon and Mirella have created a "village of unusual roadside attractions" inspired by a documentary we watched last night at a hotel. Their version is constructed of pinecones, dirt, and moss. They have also designed a trap to catch the "clean-up fairy," which sometimes visits at night and hides things that the kids haven't put away properly.

I have napped, and slept hard. Michael is napping now on the hammock under a blanket and a slow sprinkle of rain.

August 5.

Thunder in the mountains sounds like the gods bowling—loud booms— raindrops on our tent like corn kernels popping. I lay awake awhile last night worried about the tall trees toppling onto our tent, then worried about earthquakes until I finally fell asleep, only to be greeted by strange dreams. I woke in the middle of the night to utter silence after the rain. Branch shadows made by moonlight danced on our thin walls. This morning we are slow rising, and the kids and I cuddle and play "Go Fish," while Michael starts cooking pancakes.

Afternoon.

In *Journal of a Solitude*, May Sarton writes, "I can go up to Heaven and down to Hell in an hour..."[21] That's how I feel right now—just an hour ago reveling in how jovially we inhabited this campsite during the morning, basking in the heavenly beauty around us, everyone peacefully occupied—and now I feel anxious and overwhelmed. One of our children grew angry and loud and was inexplicably determined to prevent me from resting in the hammock. I sat alone on a rock after that and tried to meditate for a few minutes. Said child received a time-out in the tent from Michael.

---

[21] May.Sarton, *Journal of a Solitude*. (New York: W.W. Norton & Company, 1973), p. 12.

I revisit the hammock and ponder the giant trees swaying in the wind. Firs? Spruce? Then, I fall out of the hammock, rope burning tender flesh near my left armpit. I feel like I am swinging in Hell.

August 6. Transfiguration.

I woke many times overnight. Once, Michael and I were both awake, and we crawled out of the tent and stared up at puffs of clouds gliding across the inky sky, backlit by an unnaturally bright moon. The silence was almost total; no animal sounds. However, later, closer to dawn, barks and howls of a lone coyote were my alarm clock. For a good five minutes, she called out the morning, until interrupted by a passing vehicle, and presumably went about her day. On this final waking, I am huddled under a pile of sleeping bags, propped against my Therm-a-Rest chair and a few camp pillows. My feet are warm; my shoulder and neck muscles are sore from a night of ground sleeping and battling my consciousness in dreams. A small choir of birds chortles outside—jays, chickadees—with a background chorus of bees and flies.

Michael is working in the camp kitchen; eggs sizzle on the stove. The kids are beginning their morning play, using the ropes they found "for free" at a neighboring campsite yesterday, to make climbing harnesses and mazes

Afternoon.

Mirella speaks sometimes with beautiful metaphors.

Of the nectarine Michael sliced: "look at that pattern you are making! It looks like the Earth with its crest!" [crust?]

Of sunlight filtered through campfire smoke: "look—the sun is coming down—it looks like water flowing!"

Evening.

Campground dirt. It is ashy and thick, a powdery layer that coats and makes slippery feet, so that the kids prefer to run around without shoes and look like urchins. The brown powder of fire-ash coats their hands; conifer sap cements grime to small hands. Tiny coal miners. I find hidden treasures in this duff at abandoned campsites: two tiny plastic magnifying glasses that the children quickly add to the cache of treasures in the car, then forget, a worn poker chip under our picnic table, assorted bottle caps, a two-inch piece of black webbing, blue and black feathers of a Stellar's Jay.

We require time like this—a space away from mechanization and European standards of perfection. My greatest pleasure today has been washing a batch of laundry: dirty underwear, washbasin, soap, water from the pump by the pit toilets. There is no electricity here, except for the batteries in our headlamps and lanterns. Mirella makes fairy houses and a stick broom with pine boughs held together with long grasses, tied with Michael's assistance.

We forget how much we need to feel resilient and self-reliant by making things, doing the tasks of the household with such simplicity instead of fretting over an instruction manual or calling the repairperson. Here, the stereo plays bird song, squirrel chatter, and whispering tree branches. No fussing with my iPod and which playlist to choose. The playground is right out the tent door—logs, boulders, dirt, grass. Warmth comes from the evening fire and from being nestled together in warm sleeping bags.

Yet, this off-grid life is not all an idyll. Everything takes longer. Time seems to slow down, and that takes some adjustment. Frustrations flare as we relearn how to be self-sufficient, how to be quiet and amuse ourselves. Freshly rinsed plates drop onto the dusty earth and have to be rewashed in water that has to be hauled uphill. A knee scrapes on granite, and tears must be soothed. So that our food won't spoil, we have to travel an hour to buy ice to refill our cooler. But, even these "hardships" teach us more about ourselves and our limits, and how we so often underestimate them.

August 7.

The half moon is high in a clear sky as I mix our breakfast cereal and distribute portions into our "travel bowls." I think for a brief moment that it's too bad Pop-Tarts aren't nutritionally sound as I toss a handful of frozen blueberries into each bowl with fingers numb from the cold. The kids are tucked into their car seats, still in pajamas, ready for this early morning departure. Michael pushes and shoves the sleeping bags into the trunk, which groans and heaves under the weight of his administrations like a squeaky, old mattress. I worry about Michael's back—and his mood.

Last night the kids woke requesting water at around 2 a.m. I lay awake for a few hours planning how to publish *Boats without Oars* as a book, giving in to the complete stillness, watching moon shadows on the tent wall.

Yesterday, we explored a large, granite outcrop that spans several campsites across from ours, and found three or four perfectly round, bored-out cylinders. Ancient Miwok grinding holes? Metates? I would like to photograph them in this early light.

Photo: Kristin Carroccino. Urchin feet. Stanislaus National Forest, California. August 2012.

Methods and Tools Revisited, Some Conclusions, and More about Narrative Leadership. *Michael*

Photo: Kristin Carroccino. Colorado hospitality from the Boones. August 2012.

Tonight we are staying in a remote cabin in the San Juan Mountains of Colorado with friends, watching a beautiful sunset, and enjoying wonderful food. We have been staying here for several days while I write a final paper for the academic side of *Boats without Oars*.

I am using the work of *Boats without Oars* as the basis for an independent study for class credit toward my seminary education. My initial hope was to find some way to integrate the theoretical world of my class work with the actual world I would experience on the road. As I talked to my professors and honed my grant applications, a few key themes cropped up that would ultimately shape the project both academically and experientially: Narrative Theory, evangelism, and Appreciative Inquiry. Essentially, I am collecting stories and combing through them for good news about the character and possibilities of the Episcopal Church. I am not disappointed; there is much to tell. The scholarly side of my work has helped me to keep my eyes and ears open for deeper trends and subtleties in the stories I have heard.

More than anything else I have encountered in seminary, Narrative Theory helps me tie the disparate strands of parish life into a holistic picture. Essentially, narrative—or storytelling—is central to the ways in which we experience our lives and make meaning from them. By listening to the stories that a person tells, or that a whole group of people tell, or paying close attention to the stories of a faith tradition, one can begin to get a sense of the ways in which they interpret the world, and the resulting possibilities and limitations they create for themselves. My early thinking for *Boats without Oars* was to listen to the kinds of stories that people tell about church and reflect on the deeper themes endemic to each person and community. As I progressed, I learned that capturing the zeitgeist of an entire community would take a much larger sample size. Even so, I learned a great deal by just listening to a few of the stories in each church and reflecting on the collective responses given during the participants' interviews. This snapshot of seven types of churches gave me new ways to think about the larger whole of the Episcopal Church.

- 185 -

I was surprised by the connection between a narrative understanding of faith communities and the practice/concept of evangelism, which is, after all, about how we tell our stories. As I plumbed this relationship further, my work took on a new character and theological significance. As I have traveled around the country, I have become aware of how crucially linked the Good News is with the themes we portray in our storytelling as a people. For example, a church with a self-perception as being "stuck" or "in decline" is not really displaying much in the way of "good news" within their community. Evangelism, then, is much larger than the popular understanding we tend to accept today; our faith story and how we tell it, can and will determine to a significant extent the possibilities, strengths, and limitations of our distinct communities.

Another highly valuable tool in my seminary studies is Appreciative Inquiry. This type of research takes a very different tack than most types of questioning in parish work. Rather than searching for dysfunction or zeroing in upon limitations or weaknesses in a congregation's makeup, Appreciative Inquiry instead assumes the natural capacity of any group to function at its peak, and then sets about to discover how that might look. Thus, the interview questions I used were very open-ended and centered upon the unique experience of each individual within the congregation. I asked participants in what ways their church facilitated their own spiritual journey, what relationships in the church looked like at their best, and what their church had to offer the outside community (I modified this later in the project: I asked how the church had prepared them to be a minister in their daily lives). This set of questions produced results, which, while difficult to quantify or group in any particular form, were nonetheless fascinating when taken as a whole. I learned a great deal about the spiritual lives of many individuals, and discovered some of the things that make the Episcopal Church such a unique tradition in our country.

My other questions addressed themes of mission, hope, and evangelism. Again, I was surprised by what I learned when posing these questions to a large number of people. Mostly, answers reflected a kind of microcosm of each personal faith journey. For example, people who love studying the intersection of science and religion tend to think of church as a place to contemplate the deep mysteries of life. I started my work in anticipation of discovering what factors help bind people together to reach outside their communities, and hoped to find that communities could be visionary and cohesive regardless of leadership or structure. What I found was a much more complex picture than I expected, and over the course of the summer, my goals and my deeper questions have changed to reflect this.

Each parish I visited exemplified some aspect of what I've learned from my reading of Narrative Leadership over the summer. I chose Church of the Epiphany in South Haven, Michigan, St. David's on-the-Hill in Cranston, Rhode Island, and Epiphany Parish in Seattle as the three churches that seemed best suited for deeper reflection. These three parishes differ significantly in both makeup and leadership, and they serve to illustrate well the centrality of narrative in the life of a parish.

Church of the Epiphany, South Haven, Michigan.

Church of the Epiphany was the one of the smallest churches I visited, and because of their recent history, they had the most unified understanding of themselves. The people I interviewed based their spirituality almost equally upon the "porous" identity of the church and the open and vulnerable leadership style of the rector. They tended to see their spiritual journey as open-ended, risky, and exciting, and they had high tolerance for ambiguity and anxiety. Every one of them mentioned radical hospitality as a keystone to their communal identity. In short, they saw themselves on a shared journey of spiritual transformation, and they were working hard to include anyone who might want to benefit from their experience.

What are the seeds that grow such fruit? Their experience incorporates narrative on a variety of levels: first, they have an incredibly unifying event in their recent past—twenty of them linked arms and refused to let the church die. This is a story that practically tells itself, and a story that many Episcopalians are very familiar with, but it is no guarantee of the kind of transformation that this church has undergone. Another crucial ingredient is that these are all people who have shared their *individual stories* with one another in a safe environment. Their rector, Fr. Michael Ryan, a recovering alcoholic with no hesitancy about expressing his shortcomings, has much experience with fostering an environment in which people can be gentle with one another. Under his capable facilitation, church members participated in a program that allowed them to be vulnerable and to discuss the things in their lives that mattered most. They came out of the conversations feeling both bound in unity and supportive of one another in their various spiritual journeys. This congregation can talk openly about their struggles and triumphs of faith without fears of being ignored or slighted.

Church of the Epiphany has a very functional and tight-knit narrative structure. Each member's personal narrative has a place in the larger story of the church, and the themes found in common are what define the church as a whole. As an outsider, I could see this clearly: the parish is in a place of healing and growth, and the way they tell the story of the recent break-up shows this clearly. Members do not harbor any grudges or focus on any of the details; it is simply a plain fact for them that eighty percent of the church left. What they emphasize instead is the dying that they, the remaining people, needed to do in order for God to do something new in their midst, and the transformation that they have experienced as a community since that time.

St David's on-the-Hill, Cranston, Rhode Island.

St. David's is more midsized and well established than Church of the Epiphany. This is a congregation with a strong foundation and broad resources, but decline hangs heavy in the air. Most of the community discussion seems to center around the proposed merger with another church, and parishioners spend much energy and anxiety contemplating a merger's merit and possibilities. In a similar vein, there is significant negative talk about St. David's location and their building. No bus lines serve the immediate area, and the church is located on a residential street that gets little traffic. Nearly everyone I talked to made some mention of the building as a liability. Yet they know there is more to their story.

In interviews with parishioners, I heard several stories that didn't fit the dominant theme of worry. I learned how the church has a history of helping immigrant families integrate into the community. There were many stories about the strength and size of their youth program in comparison to other churches. Others explained how people in this parish rely on one another and for the impoverished in their community during hard times. Many interviewees told stories of the St. David's of the past, and recast the church as a bustling community center with events like basketball games and live theater. One of my favorite stories involved Ray, a man who spent decades telling Bible stories to the congregation's children every Sunday, eventually teaching almost three generations of parishioners. St. David's on-the-Hill has a fantastic history and a wealth of viable ministry.

A few key ideas from Narrative Theory are apparent in this congregation. The dominant narrative is one of anxiety and uncertainty; no one story seems to account for how things came to be as they are, and no clear future presents itself. Thankfully, there are myriad alternative stories to choose from, as mentioned above. Overall, the people at the church identify themselves as being well able to ask difficult questions, just like their priest, Rev. Peter Lane. The challenge for this group seems to be how best to ask these questions in an open, safe setting, and in a way that moves them closer to one another and to a communal understanding of their identity and their goals.

Epiphany Parish, Seattle, Washington.

Epiphany Parish is the largest church I visited, and had the energy to match their size. Much of Epiphany's identity centers on the arrival of their current rector, Rev. Doyt Conn, four years ago, when the church began growing after a long period of decline. Because of its large size, the dynamics are different from the other churches I visited. People don't refer to the church as a family, and often they do not know everyone else around them. The worship service was much more central to how this group understood itself as an entity, and their level of participation was impressive. What I found surprising in my discussions were the many mentions that people made to various individual spiritual practices and how their Christian identity formed them as people. The rector's consistency in preaching and teaching on this subject has translated well for parishioners' individual spiritual practices.

The character of Epiphany matches its surroundings. Seattle is a place of strong religious pluralism, and a growing demographic that refuses any religious label. People in Seattle do not engage in spirituality lightly, and they want both a strong religious identity and a healthy transformative quality to their practices. Neighborhood demographics around Epiphany Parish are mostly financially successful, upper middle-class families. Thus, Epiphany strives to be top-notch in their programming for children and adults, and they are very earnest in curating their worship. The congregation considers all of these efforts to be the thrust of their outreach in community.

The leaders at Epiphany Parish exemplify some key features of Narrative Leadership. They are always engaged in crafting their story in a variety of ways. They know their history and they use it to show the positive journey the church is on and the unique identity they have as a worshipping community. They take spiritual practices to heart, and Fr. Doyt is in a constant process of linking those practices to the spiritual heritage of Christianity, to relevance and benefit in daily living, and to a healthy communal future. Leaders also do a great job of paying attention to setting, and their foci in ministry strongly reflect the makeup of the neighborhood and the city.

Beyond these three stories, I learned to quantify some characteristics very particular to the Episcopal Church. In the vast majority of my interviews, participants mentioned the lack of judgment within the Church to be of high value; they appreciate the ability to be wherever they are on their spiritual journey and still be welcomed into a community. In American religion, this kind of ethos is often difficult to find. The sacraments also play a large part in how people experience church; they provide a strong touchstone for people who are wrestling with their spirituality and a core foundation that fosters lifelong commitment. The progressive and inclusive nature of our church seems to flow out of such experiences in so many lives.

I was surprised to discover exactly how much power is concentrated in the role of the leader. People tend to use the rector as a figure or icon for their feelings about the whole of the community. Many of my interviews centered on sermons and pastoral care as keys to people's experience of church, and often the rector was the place where they put their hope for the future of the parish. As such, the personality of the priest has a strong effect on the congregation, and strong leadership and self-awareness are crucial to putting that effect to beneficial use.

Boats without Oars has provided me with a wealth of experiential knowledge upon which to build during my final year of seminary. The books I read in working to tease out the subtleties present in my interview material have provided me with a keen sense of literary and narrative themes present in the lives of individuals and communities. The larger observations about the character of parish life and of the Episcopal Church have given me clarity for choosing where best to concentrate my studies. This project has helped me to define that murky place where the ideal meets the real—where academics can really provide the muscle for a robust practice of spiritual leadership—and I look forward to continuing to explore that intersection as I begin my career after seminary.

Journal Entries. August 9-10, 14, 18, 21. Great Basin National Park, Nevada. I-15 South, Western Utah. Panguitch, Utah. Pagosa Springs, Colorado. Taos, New Mexico. *Kristin*

August 9. Great Basin National Park.

I found one of my favorite places of the summer—pictographs and gaping cave mouths along the Grey Cliffs and a delightful creek, where the children played and waded at Pole Canyon. This was such a quintessential Western setting for me: aspen, cacti, a canyon, an alcove, water, ancient symbols—all those things that best signify this landscape.

August 10. I-15 South, western Utah.

Sunflowers nod their heads in semi-trailer-created gusts while the kids scream outside the car with Michael as referee. This is the first time this summer there has been a double time-out. Our children's anger and frustration pours out in long wails. This landscape exhausts us.

August 14. Panguitch, Utah.

Ever so slowly, I am coming back into my own skin. After weeks of primitive living and a summer filled with meeting many new (and wonderful!) people, we are on our own for a few days in the desert, reading Edward Abbey, searching for slot canyons. A bouquet of rain-fresh sage and dried lavender from Washington adorn the dashboard. Miles and miles of canyons, a vast enough place to re-member me.

Mirella, after running in from outside this morning, exclaimed, "There's been a Transfiguration! Last night all the grass was green in the yard, and today there are white flowers!" She was right.

August 18. Pagosa Springs, Colorado.

We are enjoying Greg and Stacy's hospitality for a few nights. Their property skirts the edge of the National Forest. Wildfires sometimes threaten. Mirella found elk bones in the yard and took them inside to decorate with colored markers. Greg says the bones are strewn about because some animal—coyote?—drags a leg here and there and plays with it awhile, and then some other animal uses it. Bones strewn about. An elk's life seems so fleeting. Bones on the forest floor—the carnal indifference of the food chain.

August 21. Taos, New Mexico.

Mable Dodge Luhan House, morning. Michael and Caedmon are reading. Sun strikes Michael's face, and he squints and crouches lower in the worn, blue armchair. Caedmon nestles into my side. Mirella giggles in her sleep, and twitches as if she is being tickled. The floorboards creak and groan as guests with an earlier scheduled breakfast make their way to the dining room. Crows and sparrows spread the morning news outside, as the local garbage truck makes its equally noisy rounds. Today is day 101 of our travels, and the day we re-enter Texas. Tomorrow, we will arrive back in Austin. We stayed up late last night discussing our plans and expectations for the next few months, sipping peppermint tea in Mabel's living room, for all the world feeling as if it was our own house.

Photo: Michael Carroccino. Mabel's Door. Taos, New Mexico. August 2012.

The Stats. *Kristin*

Miles traveled: 15,000+, Days journeyed: 102, Churches visited: 15-20, Jars of peanut butter consumed: countless.

I have been reticent to write this retrospective of our summer journey for *Boats without Oars,* as if publishing it would signal the end of this incredible season. Transitioning from the "simple life" of traveling across the United States with everything we needed tucked around our legs or tightly compressed in the trunk has been humorous and challenging at times. The morning after we arrived in Austin, Michael spent several seconds staring in confusion at the stovetop then came to ask me if we owned a teakettle. We have used the electric variety for at least five years after donating the stovetop version to Goodwill. In fact, Michael gave me our plug-in teapot for Christmas four years ago, and it was dutifully sitting on the kitchen counter while he was scratching his head in confusion and staring at the stove!

In my own confusion, for the first few days we were back "home," I would go to the car and select one book to bring in to read at night from the small library that had amassed over the summer around my ankles in the passenger-side floorboard (yes, it took a few weeks to get the car completely unpacked), a habit ingrained from many nights spent in tents and hotels and various houses over the summer. I was forgetting I was actually at my own house and could bring inside the whole stack! It took us about three weeks to relearn how to shop for the appropriate amount of groceries to fill our refrigerator and not our cooler and to remember we didn't need to purchase bags of ice as our refrigeration system. And then there's the heat. Texas is famous for its hot summers, and it didn't take us long to remember that when one turns on the "cold" faucet, what emerges is actually warm enough for a bath in many northern states. Most of our blunders have caused us to laugh and appreciate how remarkable our travels were for our family. I remember May Sarton's words, "Each day, and the living of it, has to be a conscious creation in which discipline and order are relieved with some play and some pure foolishness"[22]

Upon return, I have thought about those ancient Celtic missionaries returning from their coracle adventures and time spent in foreign cultures struggling to reintegrate to "normal life." Of course, they were not, and we will never be, the

[22] May.Sarton, *Journal of a Solitude.* (New York: W.W. Norton & Company, 1973), p. 109.

same. We have watched our children develop new skills and overcome old fears. Michael and I have grown in myriad ways individually and as a family. We have been encouraged about the future of the Episcopal Church. At times, the seas felt a little rough, but weathering the passing storms built resilience, and we learned to trust that clear sailing would be on the other side; our faith grew stronger.

I'm looking on the horizon now for what lies ahead: maybe formatting our blog in a way that can be more widely shared; maybe writing a new blog; moving on from Texas next year. There are so many possibilities, and we are so grateful for the adventure and blessing of *Boats without Oars*. Thank you for being along on the ride with us.

Photos: Kristin Carroccino. Trees of Mystery, California. Paul Bunyan and Caedmon have a conversation. July 2012.

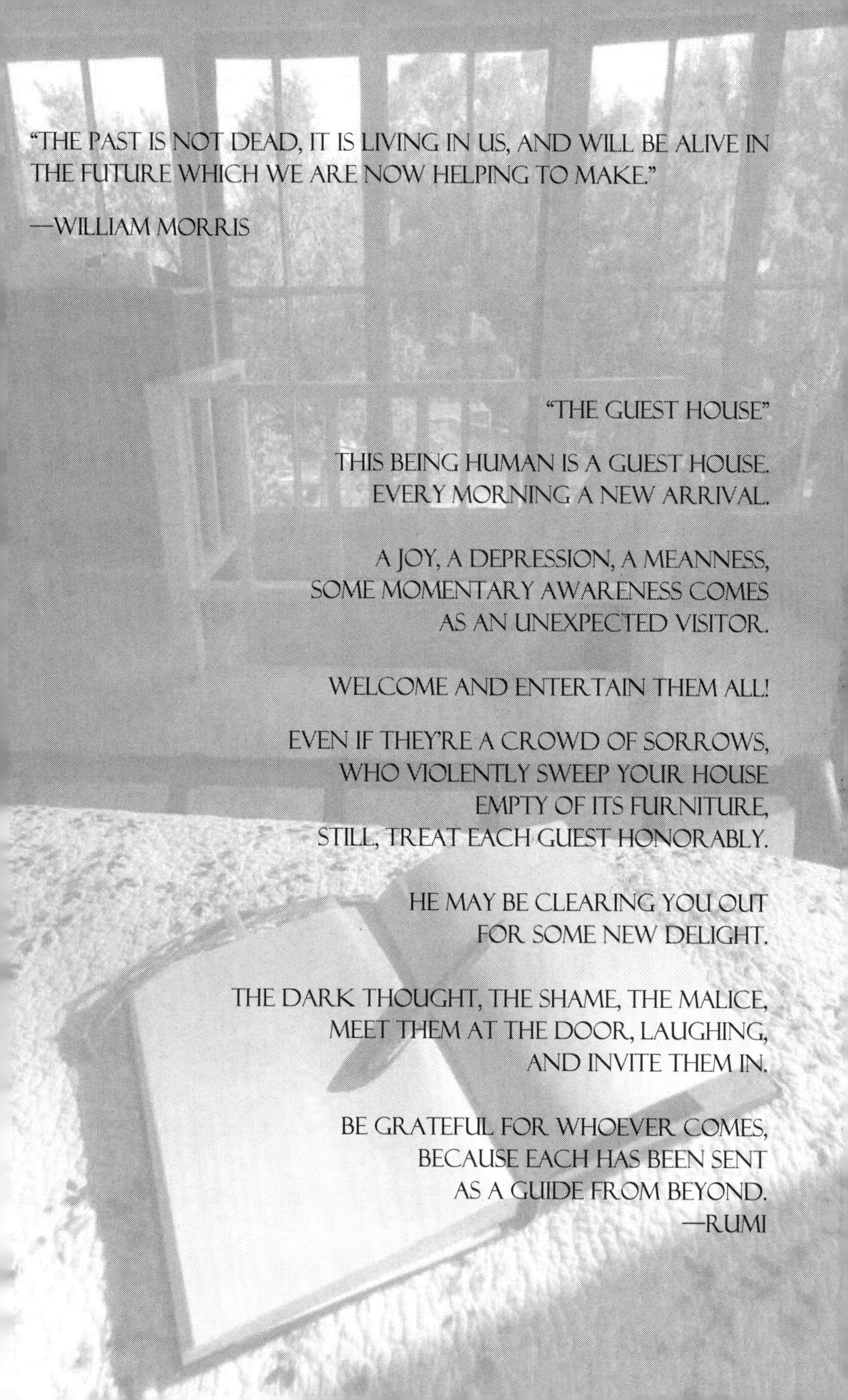

"THE PAST IS NOT DEAD, IT IS LIVING IN US, AND WILL BE ALIVE IN THE FUTURE WHICH WE ARE NOW HELPING TO MAKE."

—WILLIAM MORRIS

"THE GUEST HOUSE"

THIS BEING HUMAN IS A GUEST HOUSE.
EVERY MORNING A NEW ARRIVAL.

A JOY, A DEPRESSION, A MEANNESS,
SOME MOMENTARY AWARENESS COMES
AS AN UNEXPECTED VISITOR.

WELCOME AND ENTERTAIN THEM ALL!

EVEN IF THEY'RE A CROWD OF SORROWS,
WHO VIOLENTLY SWEEP YOUR HOUSE
EMPTY OF ITS FURNITURE,
STILL, TREAT EACH GUEST HONORABLY.

HE MAY BE CLEARING YOU OUT
FOR SOME NEW DELIGHT.

THE DARK THOUGHT, THE SHAME, THE MALICE,
MEET THEM AT THE DOOR, LAUGHING,
AND INVITE THEM IN.

BE GRATEFUL FOR WHOEVER COMES,
BECAUSE EACH HAS BEEN SENT
AS A GUIDE FROM BEYOND.
—RUMI

Boats without Oars Sermon.
Michael

Several years ago, Kristin and I went on a cruise to Alaska. We had a great time: eating, hiking, eating, enjoying the sights, eating—you get the idea. During lunch one day, the captain's voice came out over the ship's speakers to announce the day's plan. We were at the mouth of a long fjord—with a glacier looming at the head—and our intent was to take the ship through the narrow valley to the other end. There was, however, one small hitch in the plan: there were large chunks of ice in the water, and fog had been reported in the area. The captain wanted to leave us with no uncertainty that he would turn the boat around if there were any chance at all of danger. Being a native Greek-speaker, his English—while fluent—lacked a bit of nuance. He said, "If the fog rolls in while we're in the fjord, there will be NO HOPE of seeing the glacier today. NO HOPE!" I'll always remember the sound of those words reverberating through the giant ship. Even today, when Kristin and I are in a mild predicament, we will often look at one another and say, "NO HOPE!"

We've been traveling all over the country this summer interviewing Episcopalians about the church, and I'm quickly learning that when Episcopalians start talking about the future, they can sound an awful lot like the captain of that cruise ship. Author and scholar Diana Butler Bass, who has done much research of this type, says that when she talks to mainline Christians about the future, she often hears veiled references to the *Titanic*. Her interviewees use phrases like "long, slow decline" or "rearranging the deck chairs" or "too big to turn." There is much discussion these days about the future of the church—and great anxiety as well. We began this project with the assumption that *the future of the church is contained in the stories we tell about it <u>right now</u>*.

In my seminary education, one idea I have encountered repeatedly is Narrative Theory: I've studied Narrative Theology, Narrative Psychology, Narrative Leadership, Narrative Therapy—you name it. What it all boils down to is the simple assertion that you can find out a whole lot about an individual, a group, or even a whole society simply by listening to the stories they tell and how they tell them. Within the stories we tell, we can discover the filters through which we see the world, and when you add all those individual stories up, you start to get a sense of the possibilities we see before us and the limitations we needlessly place upon ourselves. And so, the goal of *Boats without Oars* is to gather a wide range of stories and listen for the themes of growth, hope, redemption, and transformation. With these stories in hand, our goal is to shed light on the future of the church as seen through the eyes of those who are already living it.

All of this started with a story. As Kristin and I were planning this project, we did a lot of reading and talking about how we tell our stories as a church—or in other words: how we do evangelism. In our research, we ran across a striking example of this practice in the history of the Celtic monks in the British Isles. So consumed by zeal were these men and women, that in hopes of sharing God with new peoples they would climb into tiny round boats called coracles, and launch into the cold northern seas without so much as a paddle to steer themselves. Their belief was that wherever they landed, God was already at work; their job was simply to join in. We were inspired by this story, and so our project got its name: *Boats without Oars*.

And now we've been working our way around the U.S. and learning the stories of the church. We've seen a church where over sixty percent of the worshippers on Sunday mornings have chronic mental illness. In another community, the church is making its spacious front lawn a neighborhood asset in a packed urban environment where open space is at a premium; and now most of their neighbors know them for the weekly barbecue they host through the summer. Elsewhere, we were welcomed in by a small church where just a few years ago, eighty percent of the members joined the rector in leaving the Episcopal Church to start a new congregation across town. The dozen members remaining banded together and embraced this death as a gateway to resurrection: now they host a rich variety of ministries—like giving proper burials for the unclaimed remains of people who have died in their city. Over half of their operating budget comes from people who don't show up at Sunday worship, but believe wholeheartedly in what the church is doing in their community. We are finding the stories we have been searching for, even here. The Spirit is moving in the God's church—and in ways no one expects. So join us in keeping your eyes and ears open, in listening for the stories that show us a future we can get excited about. After months of driving and interviewing, I can tell you this: as far as the future of the Episcopal Church is concerned, there IS HOPE!

AFTER 2012: ANCHORED (FOR AWHILE)

Boats without Oars One Year Later. *Michael*

On our cross-country journey, the broad range of Episcopal experiences and expressions unrelentingly amazed us, and the stories we encountered are an undeniably narrow slice of the whole. Each story we found had its own unique twists and turns; a distinctive narrative arc of redemption came with every new community. Further, each church we visited inhabited a particular location within that arc, a place that while fluidly connected to the whole of their story, could only provide a glimpse of their overall trajectory. Over the months following our odyssey, we found ourselves repeatedly telling these churches' stories and imagining how things might have changed since our visit. Were the churches still experiencing the same joys and challenges—or had the stories begun a new chapter?

Twists and turns abounded for our family as well. In the year succeeding our time on the road, we found ourselves adrift in a completely new way. I graduated from seminary, got ordained, and began work as a curate at Saint Mark's Episcopal Cathedral in Seattle. Kristin's writing and photography took on a more vocational status, and all four of us had to rediscover ourselves among the snowcapped mountains and island-studded waters of Puget Sound.

As we settled haphazardly into this fresh iteration of our family, my wondering about church narratives persisted, so as I sat in my office during the summer of 2013 contemplating the Space Needle, research began again. I had conversations with each of the seven rectors whose churches participated in *Boats without Oars*, and updated the communities' information to shed more light on the story it has been our work to plumb: the future of our Episcopal tradition.

St. John's Episcopal Church, Decatur, Alabama.

St. John's worked devotedly between 2012 and 2013 to create community awareness of its ministries, and to coordinate outreach efforts with the city of Decatur. Rector Evan Garner used the word "outreach" so excessively that I began a count in the margin of my notebook! The church has strengthened the connection with the Episcopal Outreach Center on their campus, providing volunteers for a variety of community programs based there.

Additionally, St. John's has initiated a formal relationship with the elementary school across the street, whereby parishioners create and staff a year-round after-school program for students. Fr. Evan was surprised with how all of this took shape: rather than picking a ministry and putting all of their energy behind it, parishioners have instead focused their efforts into understanding the deeper strategic value of intentionally coordinating the church's ministries with the end goal of being truly effective in their help to the local community.

The parish has worked to elucidate their shared understanding of the church's mission in the world by hosting a series of book studies revolving around Christian mission and theology. St. John's new curate, with all the attendant energy of a recent seminary graduate, has infused new life into this process of reflection and action. In the year after our visit, church growth was on many fronts; even as attendance stayed fairly constant, the leadership in the parish changed faces and gained energy from their shared pursuit of outreach and welcome. Saint John's, Decatur is a church faithfully attending to their inherent community strengths while uniquely and boldly expressing the mission of the broader Church.

Church of the Holy Comforter, Atlanta, Georgia.

Holy Comforter's rector Mike Tanner—true to form—returned my query quickly and energetically. The Friendship Center for people with chronic mental illness is still doing its work in the community; the church wants to increase the ministry's capacity. This is no small challenge, as the majority of its budget comes from outside the parish already. The vestry is working diligently to streamline fundraising and to imaginatively engage the community of greater Atlanta.

Both the Friendship Center and the day-to-day parish ministry at this church rely heavily on volunteer work, and they draw greatly on regional seminaries for interns. This reciprocal relationship serves to infuse Holy Comforter with fresh ideas and to form upcoming ministers in a uniquely missional environment. Fr. Mike identified this youthful leadership as the source of much energy and vitality at Holy Comforter, and spoke of one of the parish's most surprising types of outreach: seminarians from other church denominations who visit this church regularly find themselves attracted into the Episcopal Church. Given the abundance of pluck and energy suffusing its primary outreach ministry, Friendship Center, and the bold magnetism of this unique congregation, I imagine a bright future for the Church of the Holy Comforter.

Christ Church on Capitol Hill, Washington, D.C.

The "Front Porch Parish" lives on; in fact the summer "Grill and Chill" on the lawn at Christ Church has grown by leaps and bounds since we attended one of the first events in the summer of 2012. Not only do these events bring in the neighbors, but casual passersby and even contractors working in the neighborhood. Rector Cara Spacarelli said that Christ Church saw both the loss of many of the elder parishioners and the influx of several new families in the year following our initial research, and they felt the need to change and increase the church's program offerings in response. The new growth provided a particular boost to the monthly children's service, where kids gather around the altar with the priest for a Eucharist tailored to their needs and interests.

Christ Church is becoming known as a church for families with young children and for their parents. Rev. Cara is gradually retooling to provide evening discussion groups with a format based on a popular NPR series in order to provide a forum for people less familiar with the Church to take on the often-nuanced subject matter of spirituality in an environment that encourages curiosity. Christ Church is continuing their long history of being a container for the spirit of the neighborhood, and in the process providing an acting display of the possibilities of Episcopalians' adaptable expression of worship and spirituality.

St. David's on-the-Hill, Cranston, Rhode Island.

The opportunity to study St. David's on-the-Hill in 2012 was unique among the parishes we visited, because the church was in the midst of contemplating a merger. There were strong emotions and high stakes for everyone in both parishes as they worked through the process. The months after we visited Rhode Island would define for St. David's the bounds and character of a future that was sure to be exciting.

Two parishes, St. David's on-the Hill and Church of the Transfiguration, spent the months of July and August 2012 trading worship spaces: first at Transfiguration's historic downtown building, and then at St. David's roomier suburban campus. Peter Lane, St. David's rector, told me that the experience of leaving your church closed and locked for a month of Sundays is starkly informative, and gives a new lens for exploring the relationship between a community and its worship space. During this uneasy contemplation, the Diocese of Rhode Island called a new bishop, and suddenly everything changed. The new bishop felt that church merging was not in the best interest of the diocese and began working to invest energy in other areas. Talks between the two parishes were already on the verge of breaking down, and this new development put them on permanent "hold."

Leaving the merger idea behind, St. David's on-the-Hill began to embrace and enliven its geography, primarily by offering up the building and grounds for as much community use as possible. One year later, they had become recognizable throughout the city—and all because of the very building that seemed such a liability in 2012. Moreover, because of the increase in community awareness of the parish, St. David's has welcomed in twenty-five new families. Fr. Peter says that Sundays are very different now, with much more participation and joy. Most exciting for me: the still, silent bell that I noticed in June 2012 has new life: parishioners ring it so hard and so often now that "the rope comes off the track!"

Church of the Epiphany, South Haven, Michigan.

Church of the Epiphany has seen the number of people involved in their ministries nearly double. True to form, their 2013 parish retreat included people from across the faith spectrum gathered for discerning the next year's ministry in the parish. Rector Michael Ryan has worked diligently to preserve the "porous" character of the congregation by insisting that all users of the building are part of the parish and that all uses of the building are by donation. In this way, Church of the Epiphany continues to add classes and events to their schedule and draw people excited to build community.

In 2013, the church elected a vestry for the first time since the devastating church split from several years prior. Vestry members represented Epiphany's entire spectrum of ministries. One vestry person was asked to keep the church accountable to the commitments they have made to the larger community. This parish is really living the question, "how do we keep the church's identity from being a barrier to entry while at the same time remaining true to the rich fullness of our tradition?" With such an approach, Church of the Epiphany works hard at welcoming all newcomers, and they don't have trouble attracting them.

St. James Episcopal Church, Standing Rock Sioux Reservation, North Dakota.

My 2013 conversation with Canon John Floberg was perhaps the most surprising of all of the follow-ups. Not long after our 2012 visit to North Dakota, one of the three small parishes on the Standing Rock Sioux Reservation, St. James, in Cannon Ball, burned to the ground. This event defined Episcopal ministry in Standing Rock during the following year, and the repercussions were surprising.

Fortunately, the church had a good insurance policy, and generous donations arrived from around the country to cover the needs of the parish. In the aftermath, the church community in Cannon Ball rallied around the rebuilding effort: parishioners and community members were intimately involved in gathering resources and planning, and together picked a design for the new building that not only suits the community's needs in a flexible way, but also reflects their identity as Native Americans. The nave is designed with twelve support posts—the traditional number for a tipi—and a hanging canvas ceiling with an opening to a skylight above.

The excitement surrounding the rebuilding project drew people in, and worship service attendance went up dramatically. Camp Gabriel had just finished another season as Fr. John and I talked, and he is pleased with ministry on the reservation. What seemed at first a disaster actually transformed the community of St. James, and enlivened the communal connections on the Standing Rock Reservation.

Epiphany Parish, Seattle, Washington.

Epiphany's rector Doyt Conn had nothing but positive energy when describing the time since our visit in 2012. Attendance at Sunday worship was rising quickly, and deliberations were underway on the possibilities of adding more services. With such burgeoning participation, the leadership in the parish had begun to focus on the future in specific ways. Fr. Doyt described the beginnings of a capital campaign, one not run by conventional means. The parish was drawing on the professional talent and energy of their members, instead of consultants, to explore both their shared theology of stewarding a physical worship space and their hopes and commitments for a long future for their church.

Epiphany is a strong presence in their neighborhood and in the Diocese of Olympia. This church is taking part in a unique and strong vision of where their hope lies in the Church. By investing their energy in the building and the excellence of their worship, they are working to revive and renew a very traditional model of Church, but in a way that engages and incorporates the whole of their community and neighborhood. Epiphany Parish is working to move past the image of the "long, slow decline" by getting back in front of the maintenance and upkeep of their shared expression of themselves and projecting an image of forward-looking abundance and energy.

Clergy Spouses and Partners. *Kristin*

When Michael began talking about his call to ordained ministry in 2008, one of my grandmother's first remarks was, "Oh, Kristin. Whew. That's gonna be hard! You're gonna need some new suits to wear!" I smiled at her across the several thousand miles between Alabama and Washington, and encouraged her that "things are different now, Grannie!" My mother's parents spent the first halves of their lives in a rural, coal-mining town in central Alabama, and the best dishes and silverware were always pulled out when the preacher came through town and needed a meal. My father's dad was a Baptist minister, and from those grandparents, I inherited many silver-plate platters, serving bowls, and candelabra, most of which were used for the expected teas and showers my grandmother was expected to host. She was definitely the "white-gloved," southern preacher's wife that I will never be.

During my tenure in the Episcopal Church, I had quickly grown to appreciate the respectable distance held between personal and church life I observed in our rector's wife. She sang in the choir and occasionally facilitated a book group, but otherwise participated in parish functions like most of the laypeople. As Michael continued his discernment for ministry, we met on occasion with married clergy and their spouses to discuss the effect a seminary education and ordained ministry had on their family life. Overall, the stories were positive and encouraging, with frequent reminders to "set boundaries" between work and home life to maintain sanity.

Shortly after we moved to Austin, Texas, for Michael to attend the Seminary of the Southwest, I joined the current iteration of the spouse and partner support group ("SPOTS"—Spouses and Partners of Theological Students—which thankfully had replaced the former title "Special People of the Seminary.") Our group met monthly, mostly to catch up on the events of our busy lives, but also to discuss the stress of being married to a student, who was typically in a second career. We also fretted sometimes over our future role of being the "clergy spouse," "Father (or 'Mother') so-and-so's wife (or husband)." We shuddered over all the things future parishioners were going to expect of us, and our children, if we had them. A psychotherapist visited our group a couple of times and talked a lot about "boundaries," a theme that was becoming a mantra. She told us that we would need to find our "own" priest, since our spouses would not be filling that role for us; a spiritual director heavily emphasized that we *must* employ spiritual practices of our own in addition to what our clergy husband/wife offered in their workplaces to parishioners. We took notes. We started bracing ourselves for the hilarious and terrible anecdotes that were sure to become family legend as we imagined our futures.

As Michael and I planned for *Boats without Oars*, I decided that casually observing the roles and demographics of the clergy spouses and partners I met over the summer would be an important part of my discernment. What I hoped to learn was that most priests' spouses lived full and independent lives apart from their partner's career, as I anticipated doing after Michael's ordination. My grandmother would be relieved to know that my theory proved true: all of the clergy spouses I met over the summer were as involved with their husband/wife's workplace as they wished to be. I never heard any under-the-breath stories of intrigue and woe over interactions with the parish (OK, maybe one or two, but none so harrowing that grandchildren will remember them). Here is a short summary of my very un-scientific observations:

St. John's Episcopal Church. Decatur, Alabama.

I met the rector's wife only briefly. Like me, she was sitting near the rear of the nave on Sunday morning, corralling several young children. Her children were more neatly dressed and well behaved than mine.

Church of the Holy Comforter. Atlanta, Georgia.

Of all the clergy spouses I met over the summer, the vicar's wife at Holy Comforter came closest to my grandmother's imaginations of my future role. She often drives him to conferences and retreats; she was part of the interview we did with the rector, and she joined us for lunch at a restaurant after Sunday services. She was very knowledgeable of the ins-and-outs of parish life. Thankfully, she didn't mention hosting numerous teas and bridal/baby showers.

Christ Church on Capitol Hill. Washington, D.C.

Christ Church offered me the example of a priest who is the mother of young children. Her spouse is very active in parish life; fires up the grill for the church barbeques, keeps up with the parish politics. His role is similar to mine on Sunday mornings—the parent in charge of herding small children out the door in time to (maybe) make it to Sunday School. He holds a full-time career apart from the parish, and both parents share responsibility for household chores and childcare. Also, they have a live-in nanny who attends college and helps part-time with the kids.

St. David's on-the-Hill. Cranston, Rhode Island.

I did not meet the rector's wife at this parish, but learned that she has a full-time career and isn't active in the church community. The couple has teenaged children, and both husband and wife share parenting responsibilities.

Church of the Epiphany. South Haven, Michigan.

The spouse of the vicar of Church of the Epiphany is active in her parish's life, with a role that closely resembles the rector's spouse from my home parish in Bellingham. She is a leader in a citywide book group that reads spiritual books and is associated with Church of the Epiphany but open to people of all faith backgrounds. She sometimes attends a yoga class offered at the parish. She was present and obviously well-liked at the church functions we attended, and clearly loves the parish and its diverse ministries.

Standing Rock Sioux Reservation. North Dakota.

This clergy spouse is also clergy; she is a deacon. We first met at her busy home in Bismarck, about an hour north of the Reservation, where the entire family is involved in ministering to parishioners at the three Episcopal churches and Camp Gabriel. Both spouses hold multiple roles within the diocese and are often driving for hours in separate directions to fulfill their ministries. On the Sunday that we attended St. Luke's, the deacon led the music, and the priest presided.

Epiphany Parish. Seattle, Washington.

This spouse was at an all-day soccer match with her children on the evening that we enjoyed dinner with several other families in the rector's home. She is a physician, and the family appears to be busy and happy. I didn't learn much about her role in the parish. Upon reflection, though I would have liked to meet her, I am heartened that there was presumably no anxiety over the priest hosting five families at their home for dinner while the rest of the family spent the day elsewhere.

Looking back over the summer of 2012, and incorporating what the SPOTS at the Seminary of the Southwest were discerning, it is certain that clergy spouse and partner roles have significantly changed in just a few decades. Priests and their spouses view their careers and household roles like most American families; there are always diapers to change, trashcans to take to the curb, bills to pay, and times are busy. There isn't any mystical or holier-than-thou vibe among modern

Episcopal clergy families. We may talk about church and engage in more religious practices than the American mainstream, who sometimes give us skeptical looks when we talk about "what we are doing" for Advent or Lent. But generally we are working hard, like most couples and partners, to support each other in our individual callings, spiritual journeys, and ways of living in 21st-century America.

Seminary of the Southwest 2013 SPOTS in Galveston, Texas, May 2014.

Navigating Darkness. *Michael*

The very same week in 2008 that I decided to ask my priest about discerning for ordained ministry, I found out that our church was splitting up. Kristin and I had been away visiting family for a few weeks, and over a Wednesday night parish dinner, our priest told us that about half of the congregation (and the majority of the vestry) were starting an Anglican Church across town, and they had called him to be their rector. He would be leaving at the end of the month. (I waited a little while longer to pursue the ordination discussion…)

My family had been attending the Episcopal Church for only eighteen months, and we were oblivious to the turmoil hiding under the surface of this congregation. I still remember with fondness the people who departed—many of them had been among the first to welcome us when we arrived. I also remember the shocking grief and anger of those who remained. It was a painful time for everyone involved: a story that no one would call "good news."

In the years surrounding *Boats without Oars*, the Episcopal Church has been embroiled in controversy and schism. Regardless of the endlessly debated causes for this struggle, we feel its explosive effects at every level: from individual experiences like mine all the way to entire dioceses withdrawing from the national church. Even so, Episcopalians generally avoid mention of these circumstances or—especially—of those who have left. On the infrequent occasions that schism is acknowledged in worshiping communities, it is generally accompanied by raw emotion (something else Episcopalians famously avoid). This painful reality is the elephant in the room: while we studiously avert our gaze, its tremendous weight becomes the subtext for any discussion about the church. Much of the energy we devote to the Church's future (and nostalgia for its golden past) is a misplaced discomfort with our present circumstances.

This diversion is not altogether unhealthy, but neither can it be ignored. Though unsettling, there is much to be gained by turning our attention to that uncomfortable middle ground of the present. The heroes of our faith stories illustrate that God's redemptive work is not separate from the messy struggle of living in the world. Lest we are too quick to valorize the seafaring monks of the past or the change agents leading the way to the future, we first have a responsibility to remember the whole truth. Patrick's captivity as an Irish slave ironically equipped him for his fantastic success as a missionary. Columba, in flight from a brutal war that *he* had sparked, set sail to found the legendary community at Iona.

Peregrination sometimes feels less like pilgrimage and more like a tour of duty. It leaves out the luxuries of destination and time, instead provisioning our spirits with a formless expectation: an idea that each new experience can be a teacher, whether we like it or not. The inner and the outer journeys of conflict and loss in my life have created a space for understanding and vulnerability that otherwise could not exist. Sometimes I have felt stretched beyond the breaking point, unable to contemplate anything but my own anger and despair. Looking back, I see that anxiety and grief, like scabs, cover places that—with time and care—are healing into resilience and compassion.

Many of the stories in *Boats without Oars* are not tidy paths to easy vitality but very real examples of moments of grief, doubt, betrayal, and uncertainty that defined rather than destroyed the people who responded together in faith. In every case, new life sprang from less-than-ideal circumstances; pain was transformed into ministry; bad news became the preamble to the new story God was telling.

Over the weeks and months that followed the schism in my home church, some surprising things happened. Like seedlings after a forest fire, new faces began appearing in Sunday worship. Some were the faces of people I had not met in my short tenure; people who had seen the writing on the wall months before and decided to make themselves scarce. Now that the tension had boiled over, they were returning to help pick up the pieces. Other new faces were those I knew from before, but transformed by this new circumstance. They were stalwart hangers-on who kept their heads down throughout the schism—refusing to bully or be bullied, but instead holding tenaciously to their love of this community. Now they had a chance to express themselves once more; their individuality and leadership brought fresh life and direction to the congregation. Still other new faces were wholly new: people who arrived unaware of the late tragedy and were welcomed with open arms.

Throughout *Boats without Oars*, our tone has been one of steadfast hope, an essential virtue as we actively imagine the church's future in a changing world. However, difficulty and loss are also a necessary part of growing. The pangs of schism, uncertainty, or dwindling numbers may yet be part of our redemption. Greater still—like Columba's great work at Iona or Patrick's in Ireland—our suffering might catalyze us into action that transcends both anxiety and expectation. I agree with Reverend Lynice Pinkard, who said, "Part of our prophetic task is to talk about the pervasive deadness in our own lives and in our world. We are being called to revive symbols, metaphors, and rituals that can serve as vehicles for redemptive honesty."[23] Evangelism is not willful blindness to our struggles; it is instead a calling out of the deeper truth that grief and pain are temporary. So, name the elephants in the room, acknowledge pain and disappointment: like the cross that adorns our churches, they are signs that we are on our way to better things.

[Being] evangelical does not mean traveling to some foreign or "other" place that needs to be "taken." Rather it means offering an alternative in every place where the death-dealing powers rule. It means modeling alternative communities in the midst of conventional communities. We are trying to create space for the Spirit of Life amid death. We can rupture the dead culture with our presence, with our own irrepressible lives.

Jesus is not coy about the fact that the work of His disciples will be dangerous: 'I send you out as lambs among wolves' (Luke 10:3). The closer we get to embodying the real love of countercultural, feral Christianity, the more trouble we will encounter.
—Reverend Lynice Pinkard[24]

[23] Mark Leviton. "Dangerous Love: Reverend Lynice Pinkard on the Revolutionary Act of Living the Gospels," *The Sun*, October 2014, p. 9.
[24] ibid.

The Questions we Asked:
Boats without Oars Interview Questions. *Michael*

Storytelling Prompts:

Setting the Tone: Reflecting on your entire experience at [this parish] remember a time when you felt the most engaged, alive, and motivated; a "golden moment" in the life of the church. Who was involved? What did you do? How did it feel? What happened?

I was surprised to discover over the course of the summer that a sizable percentage of respondents considered their "golden moment" to be when they first discovered or joined the parish. This speaks volumes to the way we welcome people—not when they first walk in, but when they begin to integrate with the congregation. In several parishes, participants mentioned a single person or family as being vital to the experience of coming into the church.

Personal Spirituality: How does [this parish] sustain your personal spirituality? What relationships, events, or programs have best served to help you feel connected to God? What characteristics or traits do you most value in this community?

This question became the place I was most likely to hear a sentiment such as "nobody here tells me what to think," or "I can be who I am without being judged." While plenty of other events, relationships, and characteristics made the list, clearly the Episcopal Church's hospitality and acceptance are core features in its ministry to individuals.

Communal Spirituality: Concerning relationships with one another, what characterizes [this parish] at its best? How would you describe those times when you have seen Christian behaviors and qualities that have increased the congregation's faithfulness, love, and unity?

The responses to this question were widely varied, but still revealed a clear theme. What brought parishioners closer to one another and made them feel part of a caring community was usually a highly valued ministry. Some were onetime events (such as a parish reaching out to help a family in crisis), while others were ministries for which the congregation was known in the community. Many parishioners also mentioned weekly worship as a primary element in strengthening ties.

Community Presence: How has [this parish] prepared you to be a minister in the community? What has been your own most important ministry or missional experience in relating to others beyond the church? What led you to become involved?

This question changed over the course of the project. Initially I asked people how their church ministered to the community, but I began to notice a clustering of answers in each parish. People often referenced a ministry with which they had no personal involvement. After I settled on the current form of this question, there was much more variance in the answers I received. For people involved in outreach ministries the answer was simple, but others had to work a little harder to respond. It seems that regular worship and church life only take people so far in this regard. Without hands-on guidance and experience, respondents usually had a very anemic—even nonexistent—sense of their identity as ministers in the community.

Uniqueness: What do you think is the most important, life-giving characteristic of [this parish]? At its best, what is the single most important value that makes this church unique?

In churches with clear focus and high energy, parishioners were much more likely to answer this question quickly and consistently.

Short Answer Questions:
Mission: What is church for?

This question started out as "what is the mission of the church?" After I noticed nearly everyone straining to recall old Sunday School memories of the "correct" answer, I simplified it to its current form. The results surprised me: there is a strong correlation with how people answered the earlier question about personal spirituality. Unless someone had a stock answer ready to give, their answer would likely be a drastically summarized version of their spiritual journey. (For example, for someone who loves the intersection of science and religion, the church exists to contemplate the great mysteries of the universe.)

Evangelism: How would you define evangelism, and how do you feel about it? How has this church shared the gospel with its community?

I wish I had been able to capture some of the facial expressions invoked by the word "evangelism." This question affronted a few people so greatly they refused to answer. Among those who did, nearly everyone used the phrase "Good News," yet the most common image referenced was a televangelist.

Vision: Of all the things you see happening in [this parish] right now, what gives you the most hope for the future?

My original intent in asking this was to end the interview on a high note. I expected little useful information from it, so I was surprised when I began to realize that more than half of the interviewees responded with a single answer. More than hospitality and welcome, more than great music and programming, more even than families with young children, people in the Episcopal Church seem to place their greatest hope for the future on one individual: the rector.

An illustration of Saint Brendan in a boat with other monks, from the book Manuscriptum Translationis Germanicae, circa 1460. Public Domain

Celtic Christianity and Spirituality. *Jeri Ballast*

"My Druid is Christ, the son of God..."
—St. Columba

Celtic Christianity and spirituality are irrevocably bound to the early Celtic Christian saints of Ireland and Scotland. I looked up the word "peregrine" in my handy Webster's Collegiate, since the Irish evangelist monks referred to themselves as "Peregrinari Pro Christ" (pilgrims for Christ). The meaning was short and sweet: "having a tendency to wander."

My mind then wandered through various notions about journeying and the word peregrine (I always think of soaring falcons), but soon landed on a much more prosaic Peregrine, better known as "Pippin" Took, companion of Frodo Baggins on his journey to destroy the Ring.

Now Frodo did not want to leave his home; the Shire was green, the ale was strong, the food was plenteous, and to sit by the fire, reading and studying, made for a very pleasant life. But he had to go. Just as St. Patrick was called to return to the place of his slavery, St. Ninian called to evangelize the Scots of Galloway, and St. Brendan called to cast off in his small boat and end up in Iceland bringing the light of Christ to the Norse. St. Columba, too, was forced to move by evil circumstance, leaving the monasteries he had established in Northern Ireland for a rocky, yew-covered isle we call Iona.

The Celtic monks called their peregrinations the "White Martyrdom". White, because their blood was not shed (though that could and did happen), and martyrdom, because they had to leave their beloved home. Their belief was that the spiritual journey of our lives demands both outward and inward wandering, often not knowing where God will lead. The Celts had wandered all across Europe before landing on its western fringes. They knew what it meant to pick up your feet and go. It is said that St. Aidan progressed around his diocese on foot, never on horseback except in case of emergency. When you travel afoot, you see the land, the sky, the water, and the people.

Knowing the dangers that awaited, Frodo had planned to travel alone. But that is not the Celtic way, for we are not meant to travel alone but in companionship and in community. Everyone requires a special friend, what the Irish and Scots called a "soul friend" or anam cara, to help us in our spiritual journey. In ancient times, it was not necessary or even usual for the anam cara to be a priest or someone "more spiritual" than oneself. Rather, this was a relationship in which spiritual insights, growth, and difficulties were shared with honesty and good advice both taken and given. Sometimes, a soul friend is required to take harsh action to keep us on the true path. We know what Sam Gamgee endured for Frodo and we know the pain it caused him. We also know what he ultimately gained. St. Brigid reputedly said, "a person without a soul friend is like a body without a head."

Since the ties of kinship and community are very strong among the Gaels, not much happens in their close-knit agricultural communities that is not seen (and commented upon!) by other eyes. When someone's in trouble or needs help, family is right there. Frodo and Sam are soon joined by cousins, Pippin and Merry. And what an apt name Merry is! For Celtic Christians are no prigs, and felt the pleasures the good Lord has given to us should be enjoyed freely and often. Here is a great sentiment attributed to St. Brigid that well expresses the Gaelic view of God's provision:

> I would like to have the men of Heaven in my own house With vats of good cheer laid out for them. I would like to have the three Marys, their fame is so great.
> I would like people from every corner of Heaven. I would like them to be cheerful in their drinking, I would like to have Jesus too here amongst them. I would like a great lake of beer for the King of Kings I would like to be watching Heaven's family, drinking it through all eternity.

Eventually, Frodo and Sam are joined in their fellowship by seven companions, making nine in all. Each of them highlights in their own ways the best (and sometimes worst) of Celtic culture. In addition to his anam cara and his kin, Frodo is joined by mighty, fearsome warriors, Aragorn and Boromir. Both are great men, noble and fine, but only one stays the course. St. Columba is an example of a warrior monk, admired not only for his spiritual leadership, but his physical vigor. Irish and Scots monasteries were communities (townships) which had to defend themselves and sometimes even warred amongst themselves. Courage and physical prowess have always been highly prized among the Celts.

Gimli the dwarf and his ilk exemplify the incomparable achievements of Celtic art and metalworking, the reverence with which the Celtic Christians created beauty to glorify God. Old Bilbo did not go on the journey; rather, he stayed secluded and completed his book. Love for learning and a meticulous recording of both Irish myth and the classic Greek and Latin texts have given the Irish/Scots the well-deserved accolade of "saviors of civilization" during the so-called Dark Ages (the golden age of Celtic Christianity). The *Book of Kells* and the Lindisfarne Gospels are the prime examples of this achievement.

When the druid religion gave way before Christianity, many elements of druid belief were incorporated into the Celtic Christian worldview. One of the most significant is the belief in the Otherworld - the place where our spirit flies and the place where the faeries live. For the druids, the line between worlds was thin and the Otherworld was as real as the one we physically inhabit.

This notion was incorporated into Celtic Christianity in a very beautiful way. As we've said, community is vital to the Gaels. But community doesn't begin or end with those who are presently living amongst us. Rather, our relationships span all time and space, making the saints who've gone before completely accessible to us—willing to care, to share and to guide in a very real and personal way. Legolas the Elf joins Frodo's band, bringing with him the druidic love for and deep understanding of nature and her ways. He and Gimli become soul friends, each finding their mirror in one another and, eventually, sharing the journey to the Otherworld.

Throughout Frodo's travels, he is guided and counseled by the immortal elves, particularly Galadriel. In Celtic spirituality we are never alone in our journey, but have everpresent and immanent support from angels and saints, and most especially from Mary, Mother of God. Celtic culture has always respected the wisdom of women. It is said that St. Brigid counseled kings and ruled as abbess over men and women both. While many monks and nuns chose celibacy, it was not required and many priests married (at least prior to Roman ascendancy). Also, many laymen and laywomen lived in monastic communities, their dedication and spiritual contributions recognized and respected.

Frodo had one final companion when he set off with the ring - a druid named Gandalf the Grey. There are likely dozens of people who've written books and articles dealing with the symbolism of Gandalf, but I'll share my own observations, based not on scholarship, but on my many readings of the books and my own heart.

Gandalf walked the dusty roads of Middle Earth, protecting, healing, teaching. He was a peregrinari of the first order. He was a wizard and performed miracles. He knew the dangers and possibilities of true sight and sought not the gift for his own benefit. He flew on eagle's wings, just as ancient druids saw through the eyes of birds. He endured the fire and was recast as Gandalf the White. He was powerful, wise and mighty. He was the servant of good. He was the agent through which the will of the Word was made manifest to Frodo. Yet, he was not the bearer of the Ring.

The Celtic peoples live on the fringes of the world, just as the Shire lay on the fringes of Middle Earth. In the early centuries of the first millennium the western world was awash in war and chaos and civilization seemed to retreat to the distant environs of Byzantium far, far away. Yet, a small trickle of simply robed men appeared, first two Britons, Ninian going to Galloway in southern Scotland, and then Patrick returning to northern Ireland. From Ireland the trickle grew, sending men like Columba, Aidan, Brendan, Columban, and many more. With dusty feet and a few companions, these men walked the paths of Scotland, northern England, France, Switzerland, Germany, Italy, and as far away as Iceland, ministering to the poor, establishing monasteries, spreading education, preserving knowledge, and being Christ in this world.

Most did not know where they were headed when their journey began, nor what hardships they might endure along the way. They traveled light, trusting in providence to provide for their needs and trusting God to take them where they were to go. It is the pilgrimage itself that defines who we are; the journey is the purifying fire. God alone determines where, when, and how that journey ends. What we offer to God is our willingness to step out onto the path and start walking. Or, as Frodo said, "I will take the Ring, though I do not know the way."

This essay is printed with permission from Jeri Ballast from her website www.heartoscotland.com. *Jeri wrote the article in 2002.*

Celtic Evangelism and White Martyrdom. *Kristin*

Boats without Oars is a story Michael and I have realized affects us in unexpected ways. When we began searching for a theme to unify our summer 2012 project and stumbled upon the phrase "boats without oars" in Becky Garrison's book *Ancient-Future Disciples,* Michael and I were in a very liminal place on our faith journeys. We both grew up in the Deep South, where we learned to romanticize pastors and missionaries as superhuman, and to struggle mightily, and often secretly, with our own imperfections, fearful of God's wrath. When we first encountered the Celtic missionaries who launched from the shore into deep waters, unsure of their final destination, we viewed them through the lenses we held as youth. We somehow overlooked that this Celtic practice was known as the "white martyrdom." Zealous in their pursuit of Christ, these Celtic monks accepted death as a possibility, and like St. Columba (see below), often struggled openly with their human failings.

An Irish homily from the seventh century explains Celtic martyrdom:

> Now there are three kinds of martyrdom, which are accounted as a cross to a man, to wit: white martyrdom, green (glas) and red martyrdom. *White martyrdom consists in a man's abandoning everything he loves for God's sake...*Green martyrdom consists in this, that by means of fasting and labor he frees himself from his evil desires, or suffers toil in penance and repentance. Red martyrdom consists in the endurance of a cross or death for Christ's sake, as happened to the Apostles in the persecution of the wicked and in teaching the law of God.[25]

St. Columba, who fled Ireland under exile, ultimately because of losing his temper over a copyright issue and then instigating a battle that resulted in 3,000 deaths, embraced white martyrdom as penance, and sailed off to Scotland and founded Iona.[26] Expanding on the ancient missionaries' fervor, Jerry C. Doherty writes:

> It was seeking white martyrdom that led the great Celtic missionaries on their evangelistic journeys. The most spiritual manner was to put your whole trust in God for the journey.

---

[25] John Ryan, *Irish Monasticism* (Dublin: 1992), pp. 197-198.
[26] For more about Columba's story, see
http://www2.law.ed.ac.uk/ahrc/gikii/docs2/corrigan.pdf

Monks would cast off into the ocean in their tiny boats made of a wood frame covered with hides. They would have no oars and would put their trust in God. The Venerable Bede tells us of some Irish monks who sailed off and landed in Cornwall. When brought to the king and asked to explain themselves they said, 'we stole away because we wanted for the love of God to be on pilgrimage, we cared not where.'[27][28]

Through the summer of 2012, our understanding of Celtic missionaries, the Episcopal Church, and ourselves broadened. We all became more human. The passage of time since then has further honed our interpretations. The church, missionaries, priests, pastors, deacons, men, women, and children are all beautifully and wonderfully crafted by God—and our humanity is just as much about our shining moments as it is our shadow sides. When the ancient Celts took on the "white martyrdom," they surely did so with fierce bravery and holy passion, but they also just as surely left behind them unfinished business, broken relationships, or conflict. As we have learned more about the Celtic monks while preparing *Boats without Oars* for print publication, we have taken them off pedestals. We are more convinced that all of us, whether in ordained ministry or not, are imbued with the divine capacity to be heroic, angelic, and dazzling, and are also earthy humans with the capacity to be cowardly, mean, and misguided. The ancient missionaries have bestowed us with revitalized insight into our individual and communal potential for complacency and schism as well as greatness and unity.

Another interesting discovery we made when working on *Boats without Oars* is how the churches we saw demonstrating life and growth in 2012 often unknowingly modeled their evangelistic style after the basic tenets of Celtic evangelism. In *The Celtic Way of Evangelism*, George G. Hunter contrasts the "Roman model" and the "Celtic model" of evangelism. Below is an outline created in 2013 by St. Matthew's Episcopal Church in Ashland, Ohio, explaining the difference between the two styles:[29]

---

[27] Jerry C. Doherty. *A Celtic Model of Ministry: The Reawakening of Community Spirituality.* (The Liturgical Press, 2003), pp.38-39.
[28] Esther de Waal. *A World Made Whole: Rediscovering the Celtic Tradition.* (London: Harper Collins, 1991), p. 19.
[29] Celtic Roots: Evangelism, Lenten Study Series #5 (March 20, 2013) http://www.stmatthewashland.org/celtic-evangelism.pdf.

Roman model for evangelism (much of today's church):

-Cultural message as well as a religious message. Puritans wanted the American Indians to have a "more decent and English way of living." Local culture was seen as a barrier to Christian faith. Note that for a very long time, everyone in the Catholic Church had to speak Latin.

-Sequence: (Sometimes there was an extensive pre-evangelism phase of enculturation.)

1. We present Christ.

2. The person decides.

3. The person is welcomed into community with other believers.

Both the presentation and the reception are often very individualistic.

Celtic model for evangelism:

-Built on the audience's existing culture ([it is] sometimes said that the Druidical faith was the "old testament" for the Christian message).

-Sequence:

1. Establish fellowship—person is welcomed into community. Belonging comes before believing.

2. Ministry and conversation. Fellowship enables belief and commitment.

3. Person accepts Christ

Very team-oriented approach; not confrontational or lone-ranger.

St. Patrick's strategy

-Aimed at a high level of ethos (intrinsic believability of the speaker).

-High level of identification with the target community, both language and culture.

-Established small parish churches with a degree of local autonomy.

Based on our observations of a small sampling of Episcopal churches for *Boats without Oars*, I feel encouraged that the church seems to be moving from the long-dominant Roman model of evangelism, which assumes a pristine version of faith to which everyone must adhere, to a much more indigenous expression of faith that mirrors Celtic evangelism. In summer 2012, the churches we encountered that were energized and bringing new life were essentially incorporating this ancient model. When church moves into the neighborhood and meets people as they are, practices radical hospitality, and focuses on inclusion rather than conformity before a person is accepted by the community, She is a city on a hill, the salt of the earth, the light on a lamp-stand, the kingdom of heaven at hand, and Good News for our future.

Image: St. Columba on his Coracle Boat. Public domain.

Recollections from the Backseat.
Caedmon Carroccino and Mirella Carroccino

Road Trip. *Mirella Carroccino*

Rocky landscapes in the desert.
Ocean waves whoosh up and down.
Aching legs as we pass by trees on the trail.
Day and night: hours of the day we drive.

Tweet, tweet a bird sings on a passing-by tree.
Running around the KOA cabin.
Irritable Dads and hot weather.
Packing up from our camping trip.

Mirella Carroccino draws comics and loves to sew. Some of her first comic strips were created during the summer of 2012.

Memory. *Caedmon Carroccino*

Monorail riding in Seattle.
Eating ice cream by the drawbridge in Mystic, Connecticut.
Museums of all kinds.
On four states in a single circle: Arizona, Utah, Colorado, and New Mexico.
Riding the talking elevator at Gigi's house in Florida.
Yawning in the back seat while we drove miles and miles.

Caedmon Carroccino currently loves technology, especially Linux and Lego Mindstorms EV3.

Photo: Mirella Carroccino. Mom and Dad at the Oars. Lac de Roches, British Columbia. Sept. 2014

End of Summer, 2014. *Kristin*

My fingers fly across the keys, slightly calloused from hours of typing at the kitchen table next to Michael, who is adding final touches to a watercolor painting he started a few days ago during our family vacation to a remote cabin in central British Columbia. *Boats without Oars* wasn't at the top of my list for "peaceful and relaxing" activities to enjoy while on family holiday, but then again, this project has had an uncanny way of continuing to shape all of us on our individual journeys of faith and as a family. On the third night of our two-week stay here, I woke under an incessantly bright, full moon and knew it was time to finish *Boats without Oars*, tie the boat to the dock, at least for a while.

We moved from Austin back to our "home" Diocese of Olympia at the end of May 2013 for Michael to begin his job as a curate at St. Mark's Cathedral near downtown Seattle. We settled into the upper floor of a rambling house we share with, at current writing, two other families and a summer intern. We all have separate living quarters but spend time communally in weekly meals and prayers and monthly gardening days. In addition to teaching our wildly brilliant, sweet, and precocious children at home during the academic year, continuing to hone and pursue my skills as a writer and photographer, I do writing and editing work for my downstairs neighbors, who manage a nonprofit ministry called "Mustard Seed Associates." We also adopted a highly anxious Jack Russell terrier.

Our summer 2012 saga has had far-reaching effects, and will never leave us; it was truly one of those "experiences of a lifetime." I can no longer enter an Episcopal church without quickly picking up the dominant narrative themes and perceiving both the congregations' greatest hopes and deepest fears. When I meet parishioners who are asking tough questions about the future and daring to try new approaches of "being church," I am reminded of the ancient Celts again, casting off into unknown waters, and I am heartened by my new acquaintances' bravery. Photo albums and souvenirs around our apartment remind me daily of the journey we took and the hope, courage, and optimism that were constant companions.

Now we stand again on an ocean shore of sorts: Michael's curacy will end at St. Mark's next summer, and we don't know where we will next land. But that's okay. I know from my journey of *Boats without Oars* that there are many Episcopal churches out there waiting to welcome adventurers like us, and that the future of our church is full of hope and energy. I'm standing firmly on this shore, but also excited about our family's next voyage.

"So at once I realize that I am in a situation that is not sheltered and safe, for to be transformed means being open, and while standing firmly in this place where I belong, I am firmly rooted, yet never static."
—Esther de Waal[30]

---

[30] Esther de Waal, *To Pause at the Threshold: Reflections on Living on the Border* (Morehouse, 2014), p. 18.

August 6. Transfiguration. *Michael*

"Then Peter said to Jesus, 'Rabbi, it is good for us to be here; let us make three dwellings, one for you, one for Moses, and one for Elijah.' He did not know what to say, for they were terrified" (Mark 9:5-6 NRSV).

Is terror the appropriate
response to God?
Absolutely.

For we are surrounded
nowhere to run
in this deep mountain
gorge—the sky shrouded
in mist obscuring the origin
of distant avalanche rumble
and the close (too close?) sharp reports
of boulders breaking free
to plummet alongside
rushing cascades frantic to escape
into the chasm below the pass—the boundary.
Unwilling to join the deadly mad
cacophonous dash to the sea,
there is no destination but up
and—stripped of the option to flee –
ours is the persistent
slow
trudge of great altitude
becoming greater.
a divine summons? a chance gathering of mountaineers?
are they different?
My body knows only
the heightened awareness, the too-quick laughter
and quickened pulse of anticipation

Is terror the appropriate
response to God?
Absolutely.

For this *terra*—not so *firma*—
is unforgiving and steep:
unsteady to the step,
unyielding to the fall,
and uncaring to hope
or ambition.
Cinching boots and hoisting packs
we place our lives in the hands
of that which only faith
(and earthquakes, landslides, avalanche, etc.)
can move.
Is it passion? idle time? image-conscious machismo?
are they different?
my body knows only
the intensifying ache of overloaded joints
the relentless conquer of inertia
and the raw chafing of unfamiliar territory.

Is terror the appropriate
response to God?
Absolutely.

For I left the high pass
traveling alone in the blaze
of midday to climb higher still
into a cloudless sky
forsaking the roaring gorge
to spend a night exposed
quaking, restless, with labored breath.
Is it terror? the chill of nearby glaciers?
the altitude?
are they different?
My body knows only
the weary discomfort,
the building awareness that I cannot
survive long in this place.

Is terror the appropriate
response to God?
Absolutely.

For as the new day arrives
and the glorious blazing star
tints the clouds with its
beautiful fury, I know without knowing
I am no longer alone (was I ever?)
unaccountably wary, I turn and
just there, a horned shaggy beast
its black eyes fixed on mine, widened
fierceness examines me with intent
measuring my gaze, my stance
my fear
my kinship
before I am deemed a worthy witness
for its rugged hind.
And it is gone.
Is it a divine encounter? a mountain goat?
are they different?
My body knows only
the pricked awareness of being watched
the danger of mystery,
and the enfolding rush
of recognition, deep connection
terror transformed
is transcendent, sublime.

Is terror the appropriate
response to God?
Absolutely.

This poem was first published in A Journey toward Home: Soul Travel from Advent to Lent. *Mustard Seed Associates, October 2014.*

The Elegant Story. *Michael*

At the time, I wouldn't have guessed that I was experiencing a turning point. I was nervous, and more than a little irritated. The stifling North Dakota heat only intensified my discomfort as I looked across the chainsaw-carved eagle lectern at a tiny gathering of Sioux Episcopalians. I was preaching an early version of the *Boats without Oars* sermon—the story I would tell to every subsequent congregation that summer—when five-year-old Mirella broke free from Kristin, sprinted to the front of the church, and latched herself to my leg with every bit of energy she could muster.

Photo: Kristin Carroccino. Mirella, end of summer 2014

A short interruption to my homily ensued, in which I tried every parenting trick suitable for such a public interaction (a very limited catalog) to extricate myself from her tiny grasp. Failing that, I turned my attention back to the congregation and continued my sermon. Resolute, quiet, and still holding on with all her might, Mirella persevered until I finished. After so many weeks together on the road, and so much time in churches, *Boats without Oars* had become inextricable from our family experience. Our connection to one another and to the work outweighed decorum (if sometimes unfortunately). In that small North Dakota church, no one batted an eye. My experience, rather than forcing me to choose between family and propriety, became an exploration of a new sense of both. A thousand miles from any place or anyone I had ever known, I was with my people; I was home.

There are no strangers in the Episcopal Church. That's the message that carries through the one hundred days of our epic journey as well as the two years that have lapsed since. Beneath convention and ritual, political and tribal affiliation, regional identity, and even definitions of spirituality, there is a deep-seated *acceptance* of every other person as a unique and valuable individual in relation to God. While the expression of this character varies from place to place and is sometimes obscured by anxiety or misunderstanding, our collective embrace of the other defines us as a church. By our shared resolution to venerate our inherited traditions even as we bend and reshape them to ever-changing circumstances, our communion is at once limber enough to responsively absorb the winds and waves of human understanding while still strong enough to bear us up together upon the sea of mystery that is our interaction with the divine. A more rigid craft might splinter.

Narrative scholars point out that a unifying concept in their studies is that of the "Elegant Story." This story (or image, or epic) most fully characterizes the experience of a particular person or community. The elegant story is not always a happy one, and it is subject to change over time, but in general, it is the story that people will tell about themselves (or one another) repeatedly. Think of Neil Armstrong stepping onto the moon, Rosa Parks steadfastly refusing to give up her seat, or perhaps the Y2K hysteria as the millennium approached. Each of these is a story that exemplifies and contains the stories of thousands, or even millions, of people in times of sweeping change and excitement. All of us have a collection of elegant stories, and so does every church. Because of *Boats without Oars*, I carry with me a long list of such tales, and they continually bless me.

Two years later, I still share many of these stories. I remember Rev. Michael Ryan rearranging the worship space so people could look at one another, Sunday worship at Holy Comforter in Atlanta, the silent bell at St. David's on-the-Hill which now rings energetically every Sunday, the buffalo hide "Gospel book" at St. Luke's in Fort Yates, spending my birthday at General Convention. In classes at church, over dinner with new friends, in sermons, and even job interviews, these church stories have become for me a sourcebook for what our church can be at its best.

However, these stories are bigger than just my interactions with church. This journey was not undertaken alone, and it was always more than a simple research project. *Boats without Oars* is its own elegant story, one that continues to provide a sense of cohesion and identity for our family. We have our own sourcebook of family stories. We often remind Caedmon and Mirella of the time our dinner on the beach in the Outer Banks became a whirling sandstorm with wild waves nipping at our heels as we beat a hasty retreat to the car. We remember swimming in Lake Superior on Mirella's birthday, riding the Staten Island Ferry past the Statue of Liberty, and the time I separated a rib trying to cram everything into the trunk of the car. These stories have given us a memory of our family as a cohesive unit: capable, resilient, and adventurous. These elegant stories have changed us all for the better.

Photo: Michael Carroccino. Cooking dinner before the storm, May 2012, Outer Banks, North Carolina.

When I finished preaching my sermon on that day in North Dakota, Mirella reached up for my hand and we walked together back to our pew. Mirella's mid-sermon visit, while embarrassing at the time, became a part of me, a part of all four of us, even a part of St. Luke's. In that moment, I learned more about humility and about the generous hospitality of the Episcopal Church. This story, and the dozens of others I still share regularly, has become a point of connection: a place where we can meet over the familiarity of shared experience and realize that none of us are strangers.

As I always said at the end of the *Boats without Oars* sermon, there IS HOPE for the church! Our calling to evangelize means we must seek out hope in the world, weave it into our stories, and share the Good News with everyone.

Photo: Kristin Carroccino. HOPE. Lent 2013.

Resources for Long Road Trips, Celtic Evangelism, and Narrative Leadership

Abbey, Edward. *Desert Solitaire: A Season in the Wilderness.* New York: Ballantine Books, 1968.

Anderson, Herbert, and Edward Foley. *Mighty Stories, Dangerous Rituals: Weaving Together the Human and the Divine.* San Francisco: Jossey-Bass, 1998.

Baker, David. *NASA Space Shuttle: 1981 onwards (all models): Owner's Workshop Manual.* Minneapolis: Zenith Press, 2011.

Branson, Mark Lau. *Memories, Hopes, and Conversations: Appreciative Inquiry and Congregational Change.* Herndon, Virginia: The Alban Institute, 2004.

Cahill, Thomas. *How the Irish Saved Civilization: The Untold Story of Ireland's Historic Role from the Fall of Rome to the Rise of Medieval Europe.* Doubleday, 1995.

Dahl, Roald. *The Roald Dahl Audio CD Collection.* Harper Festival; Abridged edition, 2007.

Erlich, Gretel. *The Solace of Open Spaces.* New York: Penguin Books, 1985.

Forward Movement. *Hour by Hour.* Cincinnati: Forward Movement, 2002.

Garrison, Becky. *Ancient Future Disciples: Meeting Jesus in Mission-Shaped Ministry.* New York: Seabury Books, 2011.

Golemon, Larry A., ed. *Finding Our Story: Narrative Leadership and Congregational Change.* Herndon, Virginia: The Alban Institute, 2010.

Golemon, Larry A., ed. *Living Our Story: Narrative Leadership and Congregational Culture.* Herndon, Virginia: The Alban Institute, 2010.

Golemon, Larry A., ed. *Teaching Our Story: Narrative Leadership and Pastoral Formation.* Herndon, Virginia: The Alban Institute, 2010.

Hunter, George G., III. *The Celtic Way of Evangelism: Tenth Anniversary Edition: How Christianity can Reach the West...Again.* Abingdon Press, 2010.

Johnson, Robert A. *We: Understanding the Psychology of Romantic Love.* San Francisco: Harper & Row, 1983.

Lindbergh, Anne Morrow. *Gift from the Sea: Fiftieth Anniversary Edition.* New York: Pantheon Books, 1955.

Luhan, Mabel Dodge. *Edge of Taos Desert: An Escape to Reality.* Albuquerque: University of New Mexico Press, 1937.

O'Henry, Marguerite. *Misty of Chincoteague.* New York: Simon and Schuster Books for Young Readers, 1945.

Price, Roger and Stern, Leonard. *Best of Mad Libs.* Price Stern Sloan, 2008.

Sanford, John A. *Dreams and Healing: A Succinct and Lively Interpretation of Dreams.* New York: Paulist Press, 1978.

Sarton, May. *A Journal of a Solitude.* New York: W.W. Norton & Company, 1973.

Schulman, Janet, ed. *You Read to Me & I'll Read to You: 20th-Century Stories to Share.* New York: Alfred A. Knopf, 2001.

Simmons, Philip. *Learning to Fall: The Blessings of an Imperfect Life.* New York: Bantam Books, 2000.

About the Photographs

Unless otherwise noted, all photos are by Kristin Carroccino.

Title page and "March 2012:" from a pier in Galveston, Texas.

Quotes page: "Vietnam fishing coracles" by Gilad Rom from Israel—China Beach. Licensed under Creative Commons Attribution 2.0 via Wikimedia Commons   - http://commons.wikimedia.org/wiki/File:Vietnam_fishing_coracles.jpg#mediavi ewer/File:Vietnam_fishing_coracles.jpg.

"Launch:" Corpus Christi, Texas. Winter 2011.

"April 2012:" St. Joseph Peninsula State Park in Florida. Spring 2009.

"Planting Seeds:" Fern fronds, Seattle. Spring 2013.

"May 2012:" Lake Superior near Munising, Michigan. July 2012.

"A Sense of Place, Decatur, Alabama:" hydrangea near Delano Park, Decatur. May 2012.

"A Sense of Place, Atlanta, Georgia:" pottery forms at the Friendship Center arts and crafts rooms, a basement space rented from another local church. May 2012.

"Giving Thanks for Holy Trinity, Decatur, Georgia: a tree in an Atlanta park. May 2012.

"June 2012:" Lake Michigan near South Haven, Michigan. July 2012.

"A Sense of Place...Washington, D.C.:" St. Luke's Church, also known as "Old Brick Church" or "Newport Parish Church," Smithfield, Virginia. June 2012. This beautiful place is an example of how thick in detail and high in importance historical buildings are in this area, and of how confusing it is to answer a simple question, such as, "which is the oldest church in Virginia?" Of Old Brick Church, Wikipedia reports:

It is the oldest surviving brick church in one of the original thirteen colonies that became the United States if one discounts the 1639 church tower of the Jamestown Church, and is the earliest extant church building of English foundation in the United States. The church had been dated by some local sources to 1632 but published sources, confirmed by dendrochronology have confirmed the 1682 date.[31]

"Interview with Brother Curtis Almquist:" driveway into Emory House, West Newbury, Massachusetts. June 2012.

"July 2012:" Chincoteague National Wildlife Refuge, Virginia. June 2012.

"August and September 2012" Beach scene: Bellingham, Washington. August 2012. Background photograph, next page: ladder at Mesa Verde National Park ruin. August 2012.

Quotes Page. Solarium, Mable Dodge Luhan House, Taos, New Mexico. August 2012.

"After 2012:" Lake photos from Lac de Roches, British Columbia. September 2012.

"Recollections from the backseat:" Desolate Highway en route to Austin, Nevada. August 2012.

"About the Authors:" Juniper tree, Utah. Summer 2010.

"With Gratitude:" Aspen stand, New Mexico. August 2012.

"Questions:" image from the public domain.

---

[31] http://en.wikipedia.org/wiki/St._Luke's_Church_(Smithfield,_Virginia)

With Gratitude.

For the Diocese of Olympia and Bishop Greg Rickel, St. Paul's, Bellingham, Washington, Seminary of the Southwest, particularly Professor Rev. Dr. Kathleen Russell, former Dean, Rev. Doug Travis, Dean Cynthia Kittredge, Trinity Episcopal Church, Decatur, Georgia, Jim and Gaynell King, and all other churches and friends who generously contributed to *Boats without Oars* with prayers, financial support, lodging, meals, and encouragement.

For the Rev. Mary Balfour Van Zandt, who, as a first-year seminarian, knocked on our door and handed us the first donation to fund *Boats without Oars*.

For all of the bloggers who journeyed with us throughout the summer and shared their thoughts about evangelism. For all those who participated in the interviews for our project. For the churches who hosted us.

For Christina Lopez, who first encouraged us to write this book so that it would include both our travel stories and our church research.

For our mental and spiritual help "pit crew."

For Mary Radcliffe, and her excellent proofreading, and for Andrea Frankenfeld, Mary Bergida, and Christine Sine for reading the book's proof.

For the Mustard Seed Associates, who have given us the opportunity to live in a community of creative thinkers and writers and learn more about the world of self-publishing.

For our children, who remained excited most of the time during our journey, and kept reminding us to stop for ice cream occasionally and have fewer boring grown-up conversations during long drives.

For Michael: Thanks for driving to a pay phone on the North Rim of the Grand Canyon and searching for a hotel room for us when I could not bear to sleep in a tent that night. Thanks for always being my co-adventurer on this journey.

For Kristin, who always knew the weather forecast, where to find the right phone number, and rescued countless small items from the nether regions of the backseat floorboard while I was driving. Thank you for always challenging me to do more than I think is possible.

About the Authors

Kristin Carroccino is a writer, editor, and artist currently living in Seattle. She is a contributor to and editor of two books: *A Journey into Wholeness: Soul Travel from Lent to Easter* and *A Journey toward Home: Soul Travel from Advent through Epiphany*, both publications of Mustard Seed Associates. Her poetry has appeared in several small journals. She enjoys teaching her son and daughter all sorts of interesting things, especially natural history and mindfulness techniques. She is learning a lot about robotics from her son and how to build fairy houses and use a sewing machine from her daughter. She experiences the movement of Spirit most often in nature, listening to beautiful music and prayers, and reading complicated poetry and prose on the couch under a blanket with a mug of warm tea. More information about her work may be found at www.carroccinocollective.com.

Michael Carroccino is a priest at Saint Mark's Episcopal Cathedral in Seattle, where he explores ways of equipping people to live out their faith at home and in the workplace. You can read or listen to his sermons at www.saintmarks.org. As a homeschooling parent, he spends much of his free time learning about comic books and computer programming from his energetic and precocious children. Despite thousands of miles spent behind the wheel, road trips with his family rank high on his list of favorite activities. When he's not on the highway, Michael enjoys cooking, reading, spending time outdoors, and sharing blankets, good books, steaming mugs of tea, and the couch with his wonderful wife. More information about his work may be found at www.carroccinocollective.com.

BE A BRIGHT FLAME BEFORE ME, O GOD
A GUIDING STAR ABOVE ME.
BE A SMOOTH PATH BELOW ME,
A KINDLY SHEPHERD BEHIND ME
TODAY, TONIGHT, AND FOREVER.
ALONE WITH NONE BUT YOU, MY GOD
I JOURNEY ON MY WAY;
WHAT NEED I FEAR WHEN YOU ARE NEAR,
O LORD OF NIGHT AND DAY?
MORE SECURE AM I WITHIN YOUR HAND
THAN IF A MULTITUDE DID ROUND ME STAND.
AMEN
—PRAYER OF ST. COLUMBA

The Carroccino family in May 2012 at Long Creek Falls on the Appalachian Trail, the site of Michael and Kristin's December 2, 2000 wedding.

Made in the USA
Middletown, DE
21 April 2015